*Twayne's United States Authors Series*

Sylvia E. Bowman, *Editor*

INDIANA UNIVERSITY

# *T. S. Stribling*

TUSAS 255

# T. S. STRIBLING

### By WILTON ECKLEY

*Drake University*

### TWAYNE PUBLISHERS

A DIVISION OF G. K. HALL & CO., BOSTON

**Library of Congress Cataloging in Publication Data**

Eckley, Wilton.
 T. S. Stribling.

 (Twayne's United States authors series ; TUSAS 255)
 Bibliography: pp. 119-22.
 Includes index.
 1. Stribling, Thomas Sigismund, 1881-1965.  I. Title.
PS3537.T836Z66      813'.5'2 [B] 75-1096
ISBN 0-8057-7151-4

MANUFACTURED IN THE UNITED STATES OF AMERICA

# Contents

# *About the Author*

Wilton Eckley is Professor of English and Chairman of the Department at Drake University where he has taught since 1965. He has formerly taught at Hollins College in Virginia and in Ohio public schools. He recieved an A. B. degree from Mount Union College (1952), an M. A. degree from the Pennsylvania State University (1955), and the Ph.D. degree from Case Western University (1965). He was a John Hay Fellow in Humanities at Yale University (1961 - 62) and a senior Fulbright lecturer in American literature at the University of Ljubljana in Yugoslavia.

Dr. Eckley teaches courses in graduate and undergraduate American literature. He has published *Harriette Arnow* for the Twayne United States Authors Series, two monographs on e. e. cummings and articles on Walt Whitman, T. S. Stribling, and the feud in Southern mountain fiction.

# *Preface*

On July 11, 1965, newspapers around the country carried a brief notation that T. S. Stribling, Tennessee novelist and winner of the 1933 Pulitzer Prize for fiction, had died at the age of eighty-four. For many readers, including some involved in the study of literature, this name was an unfamiliar one — and not surprisingly so. Although recent scholarship has dealt extensively with the literary renaissance that occurred in the South during the 1920s and 1930s, the tendency has been to focus on a limited number of more-or-less major figures. The unfortunate result is that some Southern writers of significance have been generally ignored — Thomas Sigismund Stribling is one such writer.

Stribling wrote over a dozen novels, seven of which deal importantly with the South. His first major novel, *Birthright* (1921), was a pioneer work in the treatment of the Negro in the South and helped to form the vanguard of the southern renaissance. His other novels of the South — *Teeftallow* (1926), *Bright Metal* (1928), *Backwater* (1930), *The Forge* (1931), *The Store* (1932), and *The Unfinished Cathedral* (1934) — came during the years when southern writing was reaching toward the heights. These novels, moreover, enjoyed popular success: *Teeftallow* was a best-seller and the first selection of the Book-of-the-Month Club; *The Forge* was the first book by an American to be selected by the English Book League; *The Store* and *The Unfinished Cathedral* were selections of the Literary Guild; and *The Store* won the 1933 Pulitzer Prize.

There are several reasons for the lack of attention given to Stribling's works during recent years. First, he did not write anything of major significance after *These Bars of Flesh*, which was published in 1938. His major work came in a burst of creativity between the years 1921 and 1938. Starting in the early 1900s as a writer of stories for Sunday-school magazines, he brought his writing career to a close in the late 1940s and early 1950s by writing detective stories for the commercial pulp magazines. Second, his novels are dated; he himself admitted this. By "pegging" them on specific social situations of the time, he almost insured their eventual passing into limbo. Third, and perhaps most significant, the Freudians and the New Critics have either ignored or condemned him, since they found in his work no experimentation in style and little obscure symbolism.

I am not concerned with the reasons mentioned above for the lack of critical attention given Stribling; I am concerned with showing that Stribling has made positive contributions to the southern renaissance. To do so, I have focused primarily on his novels dealing with the South, though I do give some attention to the more significant of his other novels. Although Stribling wrote innumerable short stories of various kinds, they are greatly overshadowed by his longer fiction and are not treated, therefore, in this study.

Although I have not attempted a detailed biography of Stribling, chapter 1 covers the early years of his life to the publication of his first serious novel, *Birthright*. Succeeding chapters cover the major novels in the sequence in which they appeared, and some brief biographical notes are added where appropriate. The last chapter attempts an overall view of Stribling's literary vision and achievement. I have tried to treat the novels in question in such a way that those readers unfamiliar with them can still gain some insight into what Stribling was writing about.

I am deeply indebted to the late T. S. Stribling and to Mrs. Stribling for their gracious hospitality and their unstinting cooperation as I was preparing this work and to the Drake University Research Council for a grant to defray research expenses.

WILTON ECKLEY

*Drake University*

# Chronology

1881 Thomas Stribling born in Clifton, Tennessee, to Christopher and Amelia Stribling. Early boyhood spent between Clifton and his maternal grandfather's plantation sixteen miles north of Florence, Alabama.

1893 Sold first story, a ghost story entitled "The House of Haunted Shadows," for five dollars. Published in a grocery-store pamphlet distributed free.

1898 - Attended Huntingdon Southern Normal University, Hunt-
1899 ingdon, Tennessee. Left in the spring to help take census.

1900 Edited small weekly newspaper in Clifton.

1901 Clerk in George Jones's law office.

1902 - Attended Florence Normal School, graduating after one
1903 year.

1904 Taught school in Tuscaloosa, Alabama, to help earn money to go to law school.

1905 Graduated from University of Alabama law school.

1906 Practiced law in Governor Emmett O'Neal's law office in Florence.

1907 Worked in editorial offices of *Taylor-Trotwood Magazine* in Nashville.

1908 Spent four months writing Sunday-school stories to earn enough money to travel.

1908 - Period of wandering. Spent some time in Philadelphia and
1916 Chicago. Also traveled in Cuba, Europe, and South America. Time between trips spent in Clifton. All the while wrote Sunday-school stories for church publications and adventure stories for the *American Boy* and similar magazines.

1917 Reporter for the *Chattanooga News*.

1918 - Stenographer in the Aviation Bureau in Washington, D. C.
1919

1920 Wrote short stories in Clifton and began work on *Birthright*.

1921 Left for tour of South America. *Birthright* published serially by *Century*.

1922 - Worked on *Fombombo* in Clifton; published in 1923 by
1923 *Century*.

1924 Finished *Red Sand* in New York; published by Harcourt, Brace.

1925 - Spent these years writing assiduously in New York; Glouces-
1929 ter, Massachusetts; and Clifton. *Teeftallow* published, 1926; *Bright Metal*, 1928; *Strange Moon*, 1929; and *Clues of the Caribbees*, 1929. Also dramatized *Teeftallow* as *Rope;* ran for only about two weeks in New York.

1930 Completed *The Forge* in Clifton. Married Lou Ella Kloss at Corinth, Mississippi, on August 6.

1931 *The Forge* published; worked on *The Store* in Fort Myers, Florida.

1932 *The Store* published.

1933 - Received the Pulitzer Prize for *The Store* in May, 1933. Fin-
1934 ished *The Unfinished Cathedral* in Clifton; published in 1934. Gathered material in New York and Washington for *The Sound Wagon*. Cruised in the West Indies.

1935 - Lectured at Columbia University on novel writing. Received
1936 honorary degree at Oglethorpe University, May, 1936. Lectured at University of Colorado Writer's Conference. Built cabin on Pinetops, two miles from Clifton. *The Sound Wagon* published in 1935.

1937 - *Winters spent in Florida, summers in New York, with per-*
1959 *iodic visits to Clifton. These Bars of Flesh* published in 1938. Wrote short stories.

1959 - Returned to Clifton and lived there until his death on
1965 July 10, 1965.

## CHAPTER 1

# Tom Stribling of Tennessee

A N old superstition in the Tennessee hill country holds that whatever a newborn baby first touches will provide some hint as to what his life's work will be. Like most superstitions, this one has never been proved or disproved by any statistical study and, in all probability, is fading into an obscure corner of past tradition. Be that as it may, story has it that on March 4, 1881, when a baby boy was born in the little village of Clifton, Tennessee, considerable discussion followed concerning what should be brought for him to touch first. "Here's a pen," someone finally said, "let's let him touch a pen first." And the pen was brought over and pressed into the tiny hand of Thomas Stribling. In this instance, the superstition seems to have held true; Thomas Stribling never wanted to do anything else but write, nor did he ever seriously do anything else.

## I  A Background of Contrast

Superstitions and desires notwithstanding, becoming a successful writer involves more than merely being "born to it." No one, of course, can ever say definitively what contributes to the development of a writer; but a glance at Stribling's formative years provides some insight into his particular development. Thomas Stribling was born into, and grew up against, a background of contrast. His ancestors on both sides of his family were pre - American Revolution English settlers in the Carolinas who moved across the Appalachian Mountains into the new territories in the late eighteenth century — the Striblings into Lawrence County, Tennessee; and the Waitses into northern Alabama. The Waitses became small-scale planters who, though holding a few slaves, worked hard on their land and were much a part of it. This side of his family provided Stribling with considerable background for the Vaiden family of *The Forge*.

Like the patriarch old Jimmie Vaiden, Waits, the novelist's grand-

11

father, was a blacksmith until he was able to develop his plantation to support his family. Honorable and generous in his personal relations, he vigorously defended slavery and his own right to do as he "damned well pleased." The Striblings, on the other hand, were hill farmers and, while living not over forty or fifty miles farther north, had no slaves. Just as self-reliant as their neighbors to the south, they remained loyal to the Union when the Civil War broke out. Christopher Stribling joined the Union army and, like Jerry Catlin in *The Forge*, was one of two men in his regiment not wounded or killed on the first day of the Battle of Shiloh; but on the second day he was carried from the field a wounded prisoner and sent to the Confederate prison at Tuscaloosa, Alabama.

Stribling felt that these two "different worlds" gave him a neutral position from which to view life. "My father," he said, "was a Republican and my mother a Democrat. And I was always neutral on the point of Republicans and Democrats. And I've always been neutral on everything I can think of. I just want to look at both sides and see how and why they occur."[1] His parents differed on religion also. He described his father as a "modified atheist," believing in God but not in Christ. His mother, on the other hand, was a "modified churchist," believing in the churches but not in the ministers. Stribling described the results that these conflicting views had on him:

I was born an agnostic, as a doubter of all sorts of things. And I was rather a questioner. I naturally questioned the morals and the manners and the social settings. Most people accept their surroundings as normal and perfect and unchangeable. The ordinary person has the feeling that he is living in a stable world. The less educated people, particularly, feel that the world is stable and that it will go on as it is. They have a feeling of confidence in it. They get out and they make plans, as if there is anything that you can plan at all. There isn't, but they don't know it. They go ahead and live in the ordinary way. But I have always recognized myself as being in a world that will change and is changing. And I speculate on what we get into and what it came from.[2]

Such a background contributed significantly to the detached and often ironic point of view which marks Stribling's novels, particularly those dealing with the South.

Christopher Stribling and Amelia Waits met in Waynesboro, Tennessee, where Amelia was a schoolteacher and Christopher an unsuccessful storekeeper. Though Amelia still maintained a loyalty to the Confederacy, as indeed did her family, love was ultimately the victor; and she accepted Christopher's proposal of marriage. Broke and an ex-Yankee soldier, Christopher was not warmly welcomed by the Waits family, but the wedding took place. The young couple moved to Clifton, Tennessee, in that day a thriving river port visited by many commercial steamboats, show boats, excursion boats, minstrel shows, and drummers of all kinds. The old Russ Hotel with its ornamental ironwork never lacked for business and was often filled to capacity.

The couple's first endeavor in Clifton was the running of a small weekly newspaper, for which Christopher wrote the stories and Amelia set the type. While Christopher and Amelia were in the newspaper business, Tom, their first child, was born. Shortly after Tom's birth, the Striblings gave up the newspaper and opened a store. A typical village store, it was jammed with all the odds and ends that the villagers and surrounding farmers might need — the kind of store that one might still find in some of the remote areas of Tennessee. When Tom had reached the age of eleven or twelve, he clerked in this store; and, though the experience was merely something to endure at the time, it proved valuable later. He was able to observe firsthand the various personalities of the surrounding hill people and Negroes who used the store as a frequent meeting place; and these people, along with those around Florence, became characters in his novels and stories.

As a youngster, Tom, an avid reader, read all the books available to him — not an insignificant number, since his father, while operating his newspaper, had received copies of any books that he advertised in the paper. By the age of eight, Tom had read *Robinson Crusoe* and almost all of Charles Dickens's novels. "I would read Dickens from morning to night," he recalled. "They were the most fascinating novels to me, and I never liked any set of novels so well."[3] This love of reading, however, did not continue in his adult life. He felt that reading fiction was a waste of time "when just everybody that comes along is more interesting than the story on paper. He's a story in actual life. He's going to do something, and whatever he's going to do is more or less silly."[4]

As a child, however, Stribling did read widely; and he tried to imitate what he read. It was the day of the dime novel, and he read as many of these as he could obtain. While clerking in his father's store, he often hid behind the counter and, using wrapping paper to write on, tried his own hand at creating stories. His father warned him on numerous occasions that, if he didn't stop such "fooling around," he would be whipped. Although on several occasions Tom came near to overstepping the limits of his father's patience, the threatened whipping never took place.[5] However, none of his family took Tom's aspiration to be a writer seriously, thinking that he was merely going through a childish phase; but, when the youngster persisted in his desire to write, Christopher Stribling became vehemently opposed. Like the majority of Clifton's population, he had a practical outlook on life that placed such an endeavor as writing completely out of his understanding and made it, as he told Tom, the direct road to pauperism. Such advice, however, did little to discourage the boy. In an interview in 1924, Stribling recalled, that,

when I was a boy, I looked over my home village of Clifton and saw a few wealthy men and many poor ones, but they all appeared to be getting an equal lot of fun out of life, with the preference, if any, going to the poor; and I acquired a disrespect of money, which I think I still have. Money is nice enough, but it's no use bothering your head about it. Moreover I am convinced that few men are in business for the money. The only service brute money performs is to act as a barometer of their success or failure. One likes to make money because one feels one is getting on, but beyond a fairly low point, no person can spend money on himself without becoming absurd.[6]

## II  *Beginning of a Career*

If young Stribling did not think much of his father's advice about writing when it was given, he thought even less of it when he sold his first story at the age of twelve. A ghost story entitled "The House of Haunted Shadows," it was published in a grocery-store pamphlet that was distributed to customers free. Tom received five dollars for his efforts, and he was quite proud when he showed the check to his mother. Naturally, such success increased his interest in writing even more; for he had, in a sense, proved that he could make money writing. Amelia Stribling, despite the check, was not convinced; but she had more understanding of her son's aspirations than her husband. Whenever the boy approached her on the subject, she would say sadly, "You can't make a living just by writing, Tom."[7]

When he was fifteen, Stribling had the opportunity to become fully involved in writing. The small, four-page weekly, the *Clifton News*, had not been much of a success for its editor and owner; and he gave it up. His principal creditor, who assumed control of the paper, hoped to recoup some of his money by keeping it going until he could sell it. Stribling became the new editor and, throwing out the boiler plate, wrote the entire paper himself. For the first time in his life he was doing what he really wanted to do — write. Soon, however, the *News* was sold, and he was out of a job.

With still some hope of steering the lad away from a writing career, Christopher Stribling sent Tom to the Florence, Alabama, Normal School. But his experiences at the normal school only reinforced young Stribling's urge to write. The writing that was required of him in his courses did not satisfy him, so he began doing themes and term papers for some of his classmates. He reminisced, "I would try to write in different ways so that the instructor wouldn't know that it was the same person doing all the writing."[8] This mania for writing and the talent that it fostered brought him to the attention of an English instructor, Miss Nettie Simpson. Her influence on him was great, so much so that he dedicated his novel *Red Sand* (1924) to her: "To Miss Nettie Simpson, in grateful memory of her early opinion that the author might some day write a book, which up to that time had been held by himself alone."

When Stribling finished his work at Florence Normal in 1903, he received a diploma and two prizes — a twelve-dollar suit for his senior essay and a medal for the best commencement oration. After his son's graduation from Florence Normal, Christopher Stribling suggested that he consider law as a career. Stribling was not too impressed with the idea; but, nevertheless, his father arranged for him to talk with Bob Haggard, a lawyer in Waynesboro, Tennessee, with the hope that Haggard could give Tom some advice as to whether he could be a lawyer. After a talk of about an hour with Tom, Haggard wrote a letter to Christopher Stribling in which he cryptically stated that the boy might make something but that he would never be a lawyer. Still, the father was determined that his son be set on the road to a definite and worthwhile profession — anything to keep him from writing — and it was decided that Tom would enroll at the University of Alabama to study law.

First, however, it was necessary that Stribling work for a year to earn money for tuition; so with his normal-school diploma in hand, he sought a teaching position. He found one in Tuscaloosa, Alabama, as a high-school mathematics instructor; but, as a teacher, he was a failure. His only interest was to observe the students to see how they behaved and to try to figure out why. Beyond this interest, he had none in teaching. It was a position of leadership, and Stribling never wanted to be a leader:

I always wanted to watch leaders and try to see why they were leaders, and to watch people and try to see why they followed leaders. That is the interesting thing to me. Who's leading the people? Where are they being led? Why are they being led? Now the answers really don't make any difference to me. That's why the problems we're having today don't disturb me. It's all dramatic, tragic, and interesting. I enjoy it just as it is and I want to see how it works out. And however it works out is perfectly all right with me. I'm not trying to change it in any way at all.[9]

Unsuccessful as a teacher, Stribling welcomed his entrance to the University to study law — or supposedly to study law. Not surprisingly, however, he spent most of his time writing essays and editorials for the university newspaper and anything else that happened to catch his interest. He spent considerable time walking around in the fields and in the community, observing people and wondering how he could develop them into characters for a story; and he thought about how he could describe their faces and their mannerisms so that readers would see them as he saw them. In talking of these early days, Stribling said, "I've been trying to write — to get the writing attitude into my mind — ever since I was born, I suppose."[10]

Graduating in 1905, Stribling returned to Florence; and, through the influence of an uncle, Lee Waits, he was admitted to the law office of Governor Emett O'Neal. The office contained an excellent library and a typewriter. Stribling devoured the volumes of the library and seized on the typewriter with a hunger of years standing. The governor was only occasionally in the office; but, when he came in, he would see Stribling intently working. His first impressions were that the young man was an extremely serious law student who was trying to take notes on his, the governor's, whole library. But a little later, he reported to Lee Waits about his nephew: "Yesterday I glanced over some of his notes, and it's some sort of tomfoolery about how a boy loved a girl, and that's what he's been sweating over for months."[11]

When Stribling left Governor O'Neal's law office eight months later, he still wanted to be a writer; but he also knew that he had to earn a living. He had just about come to the conclusion that his writings would never be published with any consistency and that he would never be able to earn any kind of a living writing. Nevertheless, he persisted in his desire, not through "any strength of purpose or of character," he asserted, but "because it amused me to write and all work bored me. I kept on having a good time while I could."[12] One day a letter arrived offering him a clerical position on the *Taylor-Trotwood Magazine* in Nashville. He had earlier submitted several poems and stories to this magazine, three of which had been published. Although the new position paid only ten dollars a week, it was a step closer to writing; and, for the aspiring author, that was reason enough to accept the position.

Though he did not realize it at the time, Stribling's acceptance of a position with *Taylor-Trotwood* was an important step toward a career in writing. His particular job on the magazine was not much more than that of general office boy, but it enabled him to meet another aspiring young writer who was trying to sell a story to the magazine. In the course of their conversation, Stribling discovered that the fellow had been having considerable success in selling stories to a Sunday-school magazine. This fact interested Stribling because anything involving actual writing would be better than what he was doing, and he questioned his informant about the basic requirements of this kind of writing. Perfecting his own technique, he wrote a steady stream of Sunday-school stories, sending them to the various church publishing houses. The formula was simple — a little adventure, a sprinkle of suspense, some twists of the imagination, a lot of melodrama, and, above all, a moral.

As the stories went out, the checks came in; and Stribling soon had enough money to quit his job with *Taylor-Trotwood*. Leaving Nashville, he went to New Orleans, where, for a dollar a week, he rented an attic with cardboard walls. He remained in New Orleans for four months, and he sought during that time to improve his writing technique. His motto during this period might well have been "Write, write, and keep on writing." He devoted a lot of time to "scribbling" more Sunday-school stories, often writing two or three before he got out of bed in the morning. He also worked at training himself to originate good plots for other kinds of short stories. Drawing several vertical lines the full length of a sheet of paper, he would list in the columns possible heroes for a story, possible heroines, possible antagonists, possible settings, and finally possible complicating incidents or situations. Then, closing his eyes, he would draw a diagonal line from the upper left-hand corner to the lower right that would touch every column. Then he would write a story based on the characters, setting, and incidents connected by the line. Although a precarious way to hit upon a story, Stribling said of it: "You can't force yourself through a system like that — always playing fair with yourself and writing the story, whether it really amounts to anything or not — without getting a grip on the knack of plot construction."[13]

Writing Sunday-school stories was not a dull routine to Stribling. "I can say this about Sunday school stories," he once remarked to an interviewer, "they allow a far wider latitude of thought and philosophy than anyone dreams of who has not followed the market."[14] Syndicating his stories, Stribling was able to earn enough so that he could travel to Europe; and upon his return he entered a new field of juvenalia — stories for adventure magazines, particularly the *American Boy*. At the suggestion of the editor of this magazine, he went to Puerto Rico to seek a Colonel Shanton, a former police superintendent of the Panama Canal Zone, to write his memoirs. He landed on the west coast, and, because he was paying his own way, walked across the island to Ponce, where he found Colonel Shanton. After he had begun gathering information about his subject, the *Saturday Evening Post*, which later was to take much of Stribling's work, offered to do the Colonel's memoirs, and Shanton, thinking that more prominence would accrue to him from the story in the *Post*, dropped Stribling.

Because Stribling was so near South America, the now-unemployed writer decided to tour parts of that continent. After a brief visit to the Virgin Islands, where he took a walking tour with a white Episcopalian minister who had just lost his congregation to a Negro preacher, Stribling booked passage on a steamer bound for Venezuela. For the next six months, Caracas was his home; and two endeavors occupied Stribling during this period. Shortly after his arrival, he met an old Venezuelan revolutionary from whom he got detailed background about some South American revolutions and the part played in them by American companies and financiers. Stribling took copious notes and toyed with the idea of doing a book on the subject, but he dropped it, feeling that the result might be embarrassing because of a lack of substantial documentation. He then turned his attention to gathering material about Simon Bolivar, the great liberator. He read everything he could find on Bolivar and was fortunate enough to find and buy, at a very small price, a complete newspaper-clipping file about the revolutionary's exploits. The Bolivar material, too, he considered as a possible basis for a novel — actually a trilogy — but he dropped this idea also. His experiences in Central and South America, however, did give him much material which he used in *Fombombo*, *Red Sand*, and *Strange Moon*.

America was involved in World War I when Stribling returned

from South America. Not long after his return, he received a letter from Paul Severence, the city editor of the *Chattanooga News*, asking him to work as a reporter for the paper. "It was during the war and reporters were hard to get," Stribling observed; "otherwise they would never have called on me."[15] He was not particularly successful as a reporter because not enough creativity was demanded by the kind of writing that a reporter was assigned to do. After working all day for the paper, Stribling would rush back to his room and write for himself. It was during this period that he outgrew the juvenile story form. He wrote *The Cruise of the Dry Dock*, a juvenile sea-adventure novel that was published by Reilley & Britton, and "Tiger Lure," a long story that he sold to *Adventure Magazine*, a publication for adult world wanderers. With the proceeds from these two works, he was able to leave the newspapers and return to Clifton, where he was soon working more seriously than ever at writing.

### III   *A Plateau Reached*

At the time Stribling returned to Clifton, southern fiction was about to begin the change that Montrose J. Moses in his *The Literature of the South* forecast in 1910. All of southern literature up to this time had exhibited a conservative and quite often defensive posture — one primarily addressed, according to W. J. Cash, "to the purpose of glorifying that Old South — to the elaboration of the legend, and the conviction of both the people at home and the world outside of the truth of that legend in its fullness."[16] The local-color writers of the late nineteenth century, for example, had continued treating the South in the sentimental fashion of John Esten Cooke and John Pendleton Kennedy. Theirs was a South of gracious plantations and fragrant magnolia trees, of beautiful ladies and dashing men, of noblesse oblige and polished manners. Writing in a nostalgic mood of an idealized South, these authors ignored the small farmers and Negroes as significant material of fiction. The southern plantation, as seen in Thomas Nelson Page's popular, romantic novels, was a world where the "greater part of the life lived thereon was given up to mere living and the means of living; to food and drink and mere comfort as elsewhere, and as life demands; only it was accomplished quietly, noiselessly, without rattle of machinery or fuss or trouble, and most successfully."[17] Page did not deny that the social life of the Old South had its vices, but "its virtues far outweighed them; its graces were never equalled. It was . . . the purest, sweetest life ever lived."[18]

The southern tradition is too elusive, however, to be definitively explained in objective terms. As Francis Butler Simkins wrote, "It is like a song or an emotion, more easily felt than recorded."[19] Stribling, in an article published in *Poet Lore* in 1906, shortly after his graduation from Florence Normal, wrote of what he felt to be the sources of that tradition:

The South, that is, the Southern and erstwhile slave-holding states of our Union, has had a peculiar history. The influence governing, and the circumstances surrounding her growth as a people have been powerful to draw Southern men into close relationship and strong sympathy with each other. In truth, this patriotic feeling of Southern men for their loved Dixie took precedence over any other allegiance they might owe. Men of the North, not understanding the influences at work in the South, wondered at Southern political men in Washington, at Southern officers in the United States Army, who were opposed to secession personally, yet who, when the rupture with the North finally came, dropped all allegiance to the Union, frankly and unhesitatingly, as though there were never a question in their minds as to whom they owed their services and their lives.

The North did not understand such action, because the North did not, and could not, understand the vital one-ness of sentiment among Southrons; nor did it appreciate the complex causes at work in the South, which must have inevitably led to such a sentiment. This sentiment and relation is expressed in the political world of today by the phrase, "Solid South."

As we have said, the causes of this single-hearted spirit in the South were various and complex. There is within the South, an element, which was once the source of her pristine glory and strength, and once the source of her lamentable fall. This element worked in multitudinous ways to foster and preserve this unity of sentiment so puzzling to foreigners.

Just as the negro, in those post-bellum days, drew the South together in solid phalanx politically, so also, did the negro serve to keep intact an almost idyllic social structure. This came about in two ways. All manual work was done by slaves, and this left room for cultivating the amenities of life by the masters. Rarely has there been so brilliant, so independent, so proud a commonwealth, and yet withal so cordial, so unaffected, so democratic. If the negro labored that this society might thrive and flower, he labored also that it might be kept pure and unmixed from incursions of foreign thought and activity.

The effect brought about was quite simple. The negro race furnished a free, unskilled labor, which could never be brought to a degree of efficiency capable of operating complicated manufactures. And yet the possession of these slaves prevented their masters from drawing into the South skilled foreign labor. Why should they engage in manufacturing? The slaves furnished an abundance as they went singing about their simple plantation tasks. There were no snarled and complicated labor problems to be solved as long as the labor used was slave labor. Indeed there was every incentive to avoid using outside labor, and every incentive to foster the institution of slavery.

And further, the very presence of the slaves created such social conditions as to rebuff any attempt of foreigners to introduce hired labor. Such immigrant workingmen would not be granted social recognition, but would be classed as little better than the slaves themselves. And thus the country was set apart; and thus a unified national spirit grew into strength and marched boldly forward.[20]

As long as the South remained outside the American economic dream, the southern tradition, as Stribling outlined it above and as Page pictured it in his fiction, could have a vigorous existence. It was simply a question of time, however, before industrialism found its way below the Mason-Dixon line. And, when it did so, new literary voices were awakened — voices that would in time transform the "Sahara of the Bozart" into a literary garden whose harvests would prove to be abundant and of the highest quality. Great changes in attitudes, values, and social patterns of the South occurred, changes that, according to Louis Rubin, caused southerners of imagination and literary talent to seek through stories and poems an order that seemed impossible to discover in daily life.[21]

World War I was a direct stimulus for change in the South because it made demands on that section for both manpower and industrial production, and the industry that had begun to spring up in the South around the turn of the century greatly increased. The war, moreover, had an unsettling effect on those who went to it and returned from it. Excitement and disillusionment mingled with broadened experiences to shake ingrained tradition and to encourage new directions of thought and activity. Particularly was this true among writers, as John Bradbury has stated:

There was, to stimulate them, a considerable literary excitement in the air and the Menckenite challenge of cultural backwardness. The American poetic revival of the 'Teens had reached its climax; the Midwestern school of social realists was shocking the country with exposures of small-town hypocrisies. Particularly relevant to their own backgrounds were two much-discussed books of fiction: Sinclair Lewis' *Main Street* and Sherwood Anderson's *Winesburg, Ohio*. Especially Lewis' mordant exploration into the bigotries and blatancies of small-town America struck a responsive chord in Southern minds and offered a popular form in which to channel their observations. In 1921 the new literary magazine established in New Orleans editorialized: "We are sick to death of the treacly sentimentalities with which our well-intentioned lady fictioneers regale us. . . . We have our Main Street here as elsewhere."[22]

Stories and poems in the old tradition were no longer sufficient; old metaphors were no longer valid; and the need for a literary redefinition of the South was obvious. The raw material for such a redefinition, as Stribling stated in a conversation we had in Clifton in January, 1964, was there:

The writers from the South won the Pulitzer one time after another for quite a long time. And the reason for that is, in the first place, the South was always defensive, because it employed slavery, and it defended itself with arguments and letters. And, I mean, through careful and particular and rather intangible arguments. They had to be subtle arguments in order to defend owning slaves. So that created a precision of expression, a passionate expression, because they were defending themselves. And another thing, the South didn't have any other outlet for art. We had no art schools, and we had no dancing schools, and the only thing — the only art — that you can practice without any aid at all is that of telling stories.

And then, as I said, it's just the plethora of material that we have about these things. Everywhere you turned, it was the drama of the Old South and the tragedy of it. The writing end of any story comes from the losing side, that's the dramatic side. We Americans always write about — that is [what] the ordinary magazine article or story is about — some man who got rich, and we read that because we'd like to think that we can get rich. But that isn't the story. The story of how a man got rich is really uninteresting. There's nothing in that that would be of much psychological interest. Any man who gets something feels better. Everybody understands that. But the man who loses somethng is the man who's got a story with pathos and the human touch that everybody feels.[23]

Thus, when Stribling returned home in 1919 after his short tenure as a stenographer in the Aviation Bureau in Washington, the stage was set for his debut as a serious writer. Just as the years following World War I were years of realistic examination of the American scene for many other writers, so too were they for Stribling. He set himself to the task. No longer was he to follow the path of least resistance and write for the pulps. No more was virtue certain to be triumphant and evil to be vanquished. If Sinclair Lewis found his Main Street in Sauke Center, Minnesota, Stribling found his in Clifton, Tennessee, and in Florence, Alabama.

## CHAPTER 2

# Renaissance of a Writer

I T is not strange that the subject of Stribling's first venture into
serious fiction was the Negro; for, in the years following the turn
of the century, the Negro had become a significant focus of attention. Negro spirituals and blues songs swept the land, and Negro ac-
tors and singers found their places in the entertainment world.
Indeed, spirituals were being recognized as one of the great classic
expressions of religious emotions and as one of the most significant
strands in American folk music. The secular blues songs also received
considerable attention, particularly through minstrel shows,
vaudeville, and Negro musical comedy. Between 1905 and 1915,
four Negro conductors and arrangers — Ford Dabney, James Reese
Europe, Will Marrion Cook, and W. C. Handy — did much to give
Negro music a national and even an international reputation. In addition to music, other rich veins of Negro culture, especially in the
area of folklore, were being discovered and mined by anthropologists
and sociologists. "The Negro," in the words of Francis Butler Simkins, "threatened to become not only human, but superhuman."[1]
   Yet, with all this attention, the Negro had still to be given any
kind of realistic treatment in fiction. Only George Washington
Cable's *John March, Southerner* (1895) made any attempt to see the
Negro as more than just a stock character, but Cable lacked the un-
biased objectivity that Stribling had for the subject. Even such
novelists as Roark Bradford (born not more than one hundred miles
from Stribling's home), Du Bose Heyward, and Julia Peterkin, all of
whom were to write novels in the later 1920s dealing with Negroes,
would not treat them with candid realism. They wrote in "the spirit
of interested exhibitors, saying: Here are some very quaint Negroes
and this is the way they live, love, worship, and entertain
themselves. They are not seen as a grave social problem, a threat to
white supremacy, or a danger to racial purity."[2]

Stribling, of course, was well aware of the many problems that grew out of the complex system of relationships between Negroes and whites in the South, and the thought of writing a realistic novel about these problems had been in his mind several years before he actually worked on one. He knew that such a novel had never been written, and he felt that, when it was, it would receive a positive reception. He delayed trying to write one himself because he did not feel that he yet had a technique broad enough or an attack powerful enough to do it. Shortly after his return from Washington in 1919, however, the "punch" that he had been waiting for came. He had just finished his novelette *The Web of the Sun;* and, feeling a bit tired, he went out on the front porch of the Stribling home to sit on the swing and watch the Tennessee River. Before long, he found himself scribbling a few random notes on a piece of paper; and these notes soon became the nucleus of a short story about a Negro, a story that Stribling himself said was begun only as a "holiday stunt" meant to amuse him.

The plot was centered around a Negro, Peter Siner, who was being ordered out of a Pullman into a Jim Crow car as his train crossed the state line at Cairo, Illinois. "Before I had traveled ten miles in the Jim Crow car with Peter," wrote Stribling to a friend, "I knew all about the youth, what he had been and done and hoped to do. I felt the pathos of the man, of which he himself was quite unconscious."[3] Stribling finished the story and decided to write another about the same character, and then yet another. After three short stories, he discovered that he was really writing a "very indeterminate novel."

If the writing of *Birthright* can be termed accidental, so too can its publication. Stribling at the time had been having some success in selling short stories to *Everybody's Magazine,* and so he sent his manuscript of the novel to them. In a few days, he received a telegram from the editor advising him that the novel was indeed well written, but that it was doubtful whether he would ever find a publisher for such a frank book about such a delicate subject. In the meantime, *The Web of the Sun* had become a remunerative venture; and with the proceeds Stribling set out for the West Indies and South America. On his way he stopped in New York; called on Joe Cox, a friend at *Adventure Magazine;* and gave him the manuscript of *Birthright* to hand around to see if anybody in New York was willing to publish it. Cox was not too optimistic, but he agreed to see what he could do; and Stribling left for South America with little hope that *Birthright* would ever be printed.

Eventually Stribling, having arrived in Port au Spain to prepare for a sailing trip up the Orinoco River, called at the post office for mail and found several cablegrams there. One had come straight to Port au Spain, and the others had been forwarded there. All wanted to know "where in the hell" he was, and if he meant to accept the offer *Century Magazine* had made for *Birthright*. Stribling cabled Cox that he did mean to accept the offer, and *Century* began running the novel in serial form in the fall of 1921.

### I *Niggertown to Harvard to Niggertown*

*Birthright* is the story of Peter Siner, a mulatto who, after four years at Harvard University, returns to his home in Hooker's Bend, Tennessee. His dream is to establish a school for the Negroes of Hooker's Bend that will prove to the white people of the village that "something clean and uplifting would come out of Niggertown."[4] Peter's overconfidence, however, makes him an easy mark for the unscrupulous banker Henry Hooker; and the plans for the school suffer an abortive end. As a result, Peter not only "proved what the white village had known all along: you can't educate a nigger" (67), but he also lost the respect of the inhabitants of Niggertown. His education had robbed him of the basic pragmatism that has enabled those of his race to exist in the southern social scheme.

As Peter searches for a *raison d'être*, he is offered a position as private secretary to Captain Renfrew, an aged aristocrat and, though it is never explicitly stated, probably Peter's father. It is he who brings the doctor to Peter's mother when she is dying, and it is he who promises Peter an inheritance because "I have no other heirs. I am the last Renfrew of my race" (160). Neither Peter nor Renfrew is able to overcome the barriers of race that stand between them, and their relationship is a strained one. While working for Renfrew, Peter decides that, if he is to help his people, he must become a kind of messiah and convince them that, through their own efforts, they could rise above the lowly conditions in which they live. But because of his naiveté he fails in this quest also. Turning to Cissie Dildine, a Negress with whom he feels both a sexual and an intellectual affinity, he marries her and leaves for the North and a new life.

From the moment that Peter Siner is forced into the Jim Crow car at Cairo until he and Cissie are on the boat heading for the North, the setting presented in *Birthright* is one of monotony and depression. The little gasoline launch that carries Peter the final few miles home to Hooker's Bend, clacking on and on interminably and seeming to make no headway at all against the heavy, silty current, serves as an apt prelude to the slow-moving, convention-ridden village itself. A mean and dilapidated river town, it has a single business street running back from the river; it is populated with hogs nosing through decaying piles of garbage; and coatless and listless men sit in front of their stores. And Niggertown is a half circle of dirty run-down shanties leaning "at crazy angles, some propped with poles, while others hold out against gravitation at a hazard" (16). The ensemble reflects both a physical and social environment that, though the inhabitants are unconscious of it, has its effects on all the characters in the novel.

Jim Pink Staggs, a Negro, probably best summarizes the theme of the novel when he philosophically discusses Peter's education with some of his cronies after Peter has been cheated by Hooker and after he has been forced into a fight with Tump Pack, another Negro, over the attentions of Cissie Dildine. Staggs cannot understand why Peter's education has not worked more directly in the latter's behalf. Peter, he propounds, should be able "to beat de white man at one en' uv de line, or de black man at de udder. Ef Peter ain't to be foun' at eider en', wha is he" (82)? Simply, Peter is nowhere. He is, first of all, a Negro; but, more than that, he is a Negro with a college educa-tion. These factors together deny him any possibility of belonging either to the world of the white man or to the world of Niggertown. The white blood that runs through him complicates the situation even more. To the whites of Hooker's Bend, he will always be just a "big nigger"; and, to the Negroes, he is a "nigger" who has forgotten his place. Thus, he is isolated and driven into himself because of an ideal he cannot realize.

Henry Hooker, the banker, is Peter's immediate nemesis; sym-bolic of the new commercial South, Hooker has the craftiness of William Faulkner's Snopes. Without a qualm, Hooker can cheat Peter and then send the money he makes on the transaction to a mis-sionary society in the Congo. This ironic gesture does more, perhaps, than any other one incident in the novel to delineate the Negro's position in the social scale of Hooker's Bend. To Hooker, the Negro has no rights at all, and to cheat one is not a violation of any moral or ethical law. Yet, not to send money for mission work in the Congo would be shirking one's Christian responsibility. Henry Hooker has succeeded in relegating religion and morality to Sundays and faraway places.

Peter's education is of little help in his dealing with Hooker. His excuse that an education is not supposed to keep a man from being cheated by shysters is not acceptable to Niggertown's pragmatic populace. Tump Pack's answer to Peter is a scandalized, "Fo' Gawd, nigger, you don' know nothin'! O' co'se a aidjucation ain't to keep you away fum shysters; hit's to mek you one uv 'em!" (60). Tump's experiences, unlike Peter's, have not worked against his basic pragmatism. Tump knows what to expect from white men, and he also knows just how far he can go in seeking redress. He warns Peter against arguing with Hooker: "Look heah, nigger, I 'vise you ag'inst anything you's gwine do, less'n you's ready to pass in yo' checks!" (61).

Tump, who has just returned from the war (World War I), has been decorated for killing four Germans with a bayonet. But the irony of his decoration is lost on him: "Yas-suh, I never wuz mo' surprised in all my life dan when I got dis medal fuh stobbin' fo' white men" (12). This act of heroism is no more than an incident in his life, and he can gaily use his medal as a last resort in a crap game. Even more ironic is the welcome given Tump by the Knights and Ladies of Tabor, a Negro burial association. The commandant of the lodge, with his sword raised high, expresses in glowing language the pride that the Negro community has in Tump's heroism. He shouts, "When we honors you, we honors them all, de libn' an' de daid, de white an' de black, who fought togedder fuh one country, fuh one flag" (19). This view of brotherhood between white and black, however, is not held by the white community. On the contrary, they regard the whole incident as a kind of comic show, the highlight of which comes when Constable Bobbs arrests Tump on a three-year-old warrant for shooting craps. Even the fact that the Negroes turn out to welcome Tump rather than Peter is ironic. They honor Tump because he has risked his life for a country in which they have very few rights. He returns no different from when he left. Peter, on the other hand, returns with the goal of helping his people; but, by tacitly accepting as their own the white man's view of them as dehumanized beings, the Negroes help to negate the mulatto's efforts.

This acquiescence with the status quo Peter finds most difficult to face, and it places a barrier between him and his mother. Like Tump, Caroline Siner is a pragmatist, and she summarizes her philosophy to Peter: "Good Lawd, boy! I don' 'speck to eat whut's good fuh me! All I say is, Grub, keep me alive. Ef you do dat, you done a good day's wuck" (87). Such a simple pragmatism prevents her from understanding her son and from conceiving of any change in the way of life in Niggertown.

The difference between Peter and Niggertown is symbolized as he sits in his room following his mother's death listening to the wailing lament of the mourning Negroes. This lament "harked back to the jungle, to black folk in African kraals beating tomtoms and howling, not in grief, but in an ecstasy of terror lest the souls of their dead might come back in the form of tigers or pythons or devils and work woe to the tribe" (120). Juxtaposed against this ancient rite are the books that form the basis of Peter's education and at which he stares in silence. He has a momentary feeling that his education, a white man's education, has not really been for him. As the wailing continues outside the cabin, the black blood in him seems to rebel against what he has become. Peter is torn between two worlds, and he is unable to reconcile them.

Cissie Dildine, who has been away to school at Nashville, is the only person in Hooker's Bend who can understand and sympathize with Peter's unsuccessful efforts to better the conditions of his people. Cissie, too, however, has her pragmatic side; for, to Peter's comment that he should have been more careful in his handling of the school founding, she replies, "I'm not talking about what you ought. I'm talking about what you are. When it comes to ought, we colored people must get what we can, any way we can. We fight from the bottom" (70).

Through Cissie, Peter realizes that in Niggertown a higher friendship between a woman and a man could not exist; for there all attraction was reduced to the simplest terms of sex. Tump Pack's attack on him for his attentions to Cissie serves as a symbol to Peter of the crudity and insensitivity of Niggertown. The fact that Negro women have no great powers of choice over their suitors leads Peter to the conclusion that not until woman has complete control over her selection of a mate will any race make progress, for only woman is truly concerned with the qualities of mind and spirit. But Peter's is the view of an idealist, a view predicated on the belief that he lives in a stable world where he can make plans and carry them out. Niggertown, however, lacks this stability; and its people must remain in a dialectic position, adapting themselves to given situations as they arise. Living for the moment becomes, therefore, a dominant characteristic of people like Tump, Caroline, and Cissie. Sexual promiscuity is merely a by-product of such a view of life.

The promiscuity of Niggertown directly touches Peter when Cissie confesses to him that she has had sexual relations with a white man. She gives as her reason the desire for Negroes to be like white people — straightening their hair, bleaching their skin, and going off to college like Peter. He can excuse her action, however, when he recalls that the Negroes of Hooker's Bend were, no more than fifty years before, slaves, "without wage, without rights, even to the possession of their own bodies" (154). They had no ancestral traditions, no past. This whole situation is made even more apparent to Peter when he accepts Captain Renfrew's offer of a position as secretary, as well as an invitation to live in the Renfrew house.

Renfrew, the traditional southerner, believes that Negro slavery was "God's great lesson to the South in altruism and kindness . . . placed here in God's country to rear up giants of political leadership that our nation might weather the revolutions of the world" (155). Southerner that he is, he sees Peter as both a "nigger" and a son. He can berate education for Negroes as a complete impossibility when talking to his fellow villagers; but, when offering Peter a place in his home, he refers to the mulatto as a "man with a certain liberality of culture" (158). The barrier of color between Renfrew and Peter, however, is too much for either of them to surmount. Renfrew will not offer Peter a drink because he cannot in good conscience break the laws of custom that govern race relations in the South.

The old lawyer's affection for Peter must be carefully couched in words and actions that belie their true nature. He does not want his protégé to marry Cissie and thus dilute his white blood; but, when he tells Peter his objections, the mulatto is shocked at the old man's reference to Cissie as a Negress and at his objection to their marriage on that basis. But Renfrew persists, arguing that Peter should think of his future descendants who will grow up under a brown veil that they will never be able to lift.

This argument makes Peter realize that not only do the illiterate whites of Hooker's Bend consider black men as simple animals, but so too do the educated men. Nowhere in the South is the Negro admitted to the common brotherhood of humanity, says Stribling. Renfrew's library symbolizes the burden of the South, for its books plead against the equality of man; and the owner excludes anything that would speak in favor of this theory. Charles Darwin's work is excluded because "the moment that theory was propounded of the great biologic relationship of all flesh . . . there instantly followed a corollary of the brotherhood of man" (219).

Peter knows that there is nothing he can do in Hooker's Bend to improve the lot of his people; for, even if there could be agreement among whites that the South would benefit by a more efficient labor, the prevailing belief is that "a nigger's a nigger." Peter faces the same problem that faces America today: "The black man would have to change his psychology or remain where he was, a creature of poverty, hovels, and dirt; but mid such surroundings he could not change his psychology" (263). In this regard, the words of his college friend Farquhar seem to hold truth for Peter: if the Negro is to progress, he must stand on his own feet; he must practice individual initiative in the same way that the white man does. Yet Peter feels that his people lack "the steel-like edge that the white man achieves." Possessed with "un-toward streaks of sympathy," the Negro lacks the hardness that enables a white man to make "his very laws and virtues instruments to crush and mulct his fellow man" (290).

Peter Siner has come full circle from Niggertown to Harvard to Niggertown, and he has discovered that there is no escape from being Negro. He had returned to Hooker's Bend with the feeling that he had the answers to the "hazardous adventure called life." He cannot, however, control the forces that impinge upon him; and they bring about his defeat. These forces do not find their source in the immediate inhabitants of Hooker's Bend, though they work through them; rather, they are engendered in the whole fabric of southern life. Such a way of life sees the Negro problem not as an abstraction but as something just as concrete as any other fact of nature. And Peter Siner learns this lesson through the course of the story, and he learns it not only from the white element of Hooker's Bend but also from the black as well. Men like Henry Hooker have, in addition to social views that see the Negro as an inferior, a vested economic interest in keeping the blacks of Niggertown subjugated. In one sense, the Hookers are the equivalent of Thorstein Veblen's leisure class and thus are not responsive to the needs for social and economic change. The Negroes, on the other hand, expend all their energies in just staying alive — as Caroline Siner so sharply points out to Peter — or, like the men who loiter on the corners of Niggertown, they have sought the path of least resistance. Either way, they do not have the energy necessary to bring about any improvement in their condition. Peter sees that imposing the white man's ways on the Negroes will not work — that each race must establish its own line of development, based on its own morals, for "morals and conventions, right and wrong, are merely those precepts that a race has practiced and found good in its evolution" (307).

Stribling seems to be saying that, if the racial problem is to be solved, it will be through an evolutionary process. The answer is not to be found in the past, therefore, but in the future. Peter and Cissie are a part of this process. Being mulattoes, they are in a sense half-black and half-white. They have the crucible to put them above the slow-moving, listless storekeepers described early in the novel and above the Negroes like Tump Pack and Caroline Siner, who pragmatically accept their lowly status. By pointing to evolution as the only real answer, Stribling removes ethics and morality from the question as well as the whole idea of equality. The evolutionary concept requires a far broader view than can be found in any one period or age. On this note, Peter and Cissie, almost like Adam and Eve, leave for the North. They have a vitality that may well lead in its way to an improvement of their race; and the process, as Stribling once said, will not be logical but biological.

As Stribling's first effort at serious fiction, *Birthright* was daring indeed, presenting as it did, to the reader of the early 1920s, an unsentimentalized, objective view of the problem of being a Negro in the South. Such a novel, written in the late 1950s or the 1960s would have elicited little notice from readers or reviewers. *Birthright*, however, was ahead of its time and was noticed.

## II   *Stribling's Response to Critics*

Of the approximately one hundred eighty-seven reviews written of *Birthright*, some condemned it as pure propaganda, but others praised it as an honest presentation of the race problem in the South. Among the many letters that Stribling received about the novel was one from a woman accusing him of complete distortion in his treatment of Negro-white relationships in the South; and she went so far as to say that he was probably a Negro himself. In answer to some of the criticism aimed at the novel, Stribling wrote the following:

A number of persons have asked me for my object in writing *Birthright*. The general opinion of readers and reviewers seem to make out of *Birthright* a straight discussion of the Negro situation. Now for me to come forward and deny such a construction is rather futile, because if I could not put what I meant in the book, it is hardly worthwhile to write letters afterwards and try to explain.

But since you have been good enough to ask me just what I did mean, I will say at once that I had not the slightest intention of taking a pessimistic view of what we call the Negro question.

In my mind Peter Siner was not any Negro. He was not an X which represented his race, he was an artist and an idealist, a particular sort of human being set down in a particularly blind village of the South. In some other Southern village he would have fared differently. I am sure of that.

All of my life I have been aware of the tragedy and pathos of the black folk I saw around me. I have seen their unhappiness and their humors, and I had never read one solitary book or story which attempted to set forth that life justly. I thought I would try.

As to the moralizing at the end, I feel sure that is about as Peter would have thought. I used the customary device of giving my hero's thoughts without the use of quotation marks. A number of readers, with apparently their uncontrollable urge to make the book deliver judgment on the whole race question, have assumed that Peter's thoughts were my thoughts on the topic of the book. Some of my readers even have said that this bit of philosophy was no part of the story and should have been omitted. To my mind it is just as vital a part of the story as his marriage to Cissie. In that philosophy I was attempting to keep strictly within the psychology of one particular person, an idealist and a dreamer, a person who simply must get his theory and practice together. That is a hard thing to do no matter what color a man may be, and all of us who think are led into some very remarkable reasonings in the effort.

I am aware — now that it has been written and published — that the book will always be viewed as a generalization, and what the author thinks has about as little to do with it as what an inventor thinks of his machine and how it should be run. Perhaps the Negro is too new in literature to permit of characterization. As I have suggested, the white critics will lump all colored men together and say a Negro is a Negro just as the writers, who choose to use the black man for minstrel purposes, lump them together and say a "nigger" is a "nigger."

Personally I do not subscribe to that theory. If I had drawn Peter Siner as a white man undergoing the same sort of tragedy, no one would have dreamed of saying, "This man represents the whole white race," or "This man's philosophy is the real white philosophy."[5]

## CHAPTER 3

# Valor and Valediction

STRIBLING returned from his tour of South America elated with his success in getting *Birthright* published and eager to begin work on another novel, one in which he could draw upon his recent travel experiences. Venezuela in particular intrigued him as a setting, because he knew that the area had never been fully exploited in fiction. The result was not one novel but two — *Fombombo* (1923) and *Red Sand* (1924). In both novels, Stribling turned to the adventure-story pattern so familiar to him. These novels, however, were to be quite different from anything he had previously written. Told with detachment and subtle irony, they provide some indication of the directions the Tennessean's future efforts in fiction were to take.

## I  *Above Poverty and Culture*

The plot of *Fombombo* is pervaded with an atmosphere of falseness, the result of a technique of massed details used effectively by Stribling to comment on mankind. The falseness is often not merely the difference between fact and fantasy, as in the instance of forced labor and professed freedom; since it is more deliberate, we could more appropriately label it "the difference between truth and deception," "between honor and dishonor," or "between promise and fulfillment." Ultimately, however, this falseness extends to appearance contrasted with reality. Conveyed principally through incessant remarks by Thomas Strawbridge, the main character, about the Venezuelan way of life, the falseness is also apparent through Strawbridge's own actions (although he, of course, fails to see himself as others do), through the author's omniscient interpolations which emphasize these contrasts, and through the combination of both those elements which constitutes dramatic irony. The impression is that nothing exists without its opposite. The political, economic, ethical, and social strictures of two societies, North American and Latin American, do not blend; and Stribling does not resolve these differences.

The Venezuela of *Fombombo* is a nation reeling from the blows of many battles fought with the immediate object of overthrowing an oppressive dictator and with the distant goal of establishing for the Venezuelan people a freedom totally unprecedented in the history of mankind. With a heavy hand, Stribling spreads the satire thick as he presents Thomas Strawbridge — an arrogant, ignorant, American gun salesman who is certain that American business methods and mores are supreme in their excellence — and the intelligent Negro newspaper editor, Gumersindo, who must explain to Strawbridge the contrasting Venezuelan viewpoint. When, for example, Gumersindo explains that Bolivar freed all of South America, yet was exiled by ungrateful Venezuela and allowed to die in poverty, Strawbridge misses the point. "Well, I'll be damned!" he responds. "Freed all of South America! Say! Why don't somebody write a book about that?"[1]

Littered with pieces of broken statues of fallen dictators, the streets of Caracas signal future events in Orinoco province, where the statues to honor General Fombombo, at the beginning of the novel, are still in the making. Gumersindo can promise fervently that there is a man who can save Venezuela, because Fombombo has not yet been shot by another aspiring savior. Meanwhile, a third member of the party on its way to join Fombombo, a bullfighter named Lubito, lounges in the background with insolent politeness and absorbs all of the conversation; and he thereby disguises his intentions of becoming dictator so effectually that his position at the end of the novel is a surprise to Strawbridge.

Strawbridge finds in Orinoco province a scene unusual in Venezuela: the construction of a huge dam to irrigate a desert. Under the direction of General Fombombo, the dam reflects an aristocratic altruism which could be the goal only of an idealist. Fombombo, according to Gumersindo, will found a government based not on selfish materialism and force, but on kindness and goodwill. The irony of such a purpose becomes apparent a short time later when Strawbridge observes at close range the "living cadavers" who are building the dam. Gumersindo admits that the dam is being built by forced labor, but he dismisses such a condition by pointing out that, when striving for an ultimate good, the end justifies the means.

In Orinoco's capital city, Canalejos, Strawbridge witnesses many instances of the heavy hand of government as it stifles individual freedom; but his attention is focused primarily on Fombombo's wife. The sober, religious figure she presents in the garment of a nun — which she purportedly wears because of a promise to the Virgin Mary, who had cured her sister of an apparently fatal illness — does not deter the interest of an American salesman. Here also, obeying the soundest of American business practices, "study the customer's business," Strawbridge volunteers to accompany the army in an attack on the town of San Geronimo. He finds this expedition invested with a sense of unreality, made up as it is of a "rabble of peon cavalry, mounted on mules, donkeys, and a few horses; a motley of women — wives, mistresses, and sweethearts of the soldiers — some in carts, some riding donkeys, some on foot" (139). On the way to San Geronimo the army stops to commandeer supplies from an English ranchman who has come to hate the country. He has none of Gumersindo's optimism, and he remarks to Strawbridge that revolutions are always being started by one set of thieves after another, each promising better things for the country, but each spoiling like a bad egg. Patriotism, he points out, ceases when one gets in power.

Strawbridge takes a horse from the ranch and, as he rides away, feels a pang of conscience. Appealing to Father Benicio, a priest accompanying the army, he finds no sympathy for morals contrary to the policies of the revolutionary faction. Of his own stolen mount, the father says, "I feel it is much more comfortable than the mule I rode, my son" (151). Gumersindo justifies the army's acquisition of property by protesting that Americans respect property but do not respect human beings. Strawbridge, who would in fact sell guns to either side in any revolution, grasps Gumersindo's argument; and there is a heightening of suspense in this plot of American materialism versus Latin sentimentality as the army advances toward San Geronimo.

When the army is split into two groups — one under Colonel Saturnino, the other under Lieutenant Rosales — Strawbridge chooses to go with the latter. In the course of the attack on the city, he is wounded in the hand and escapes to a ship docked on the nearby river. From aboard this ship be observes part of the battle, believing eventually that Fombombo's army has been defeated by the federal troops. But he is surprised when Saturnino appears on the ship. The colonel explains that Rosales had gained the fort and then

attempted to hold it against Saturnino — to carry out a plot to begin
a revolutionary movement of his own. Saturnino comments with
Latin magnanimity, "You can scarcely blame a *joven* of spirit for
playing the game. If he had won . . . he would have won a nucleus
for a state of his own, thrust in between federal and insurgent
territory. *Ca!* It was quite a stroke. I think I will give the lad a
military funeral. Such souls as his have made the Latin race great"
(175).

In addition to his salesman's business sense, Thomas Strawbridge
also has the typical prudent man's opinion that a man's mistress
should be kept hidden, especially from his wife; and he is horrified at
General Fombombo's habit of going about with a mistress and of
receiving visitors in her presence. Explaining that a man cannot
smoke or discuss risque topics in the presence of a wife, a lady, the
general adds that "the Spaniard keeps his mistresses . . . out of
sincere respect and devotion to his wife" (131). Notwithstanding his
objections to the general's keeping a mistress, Strawbridge himself,
thinking more and more of the Senora Fombombo as he recovers
from his wound, eventually seeks her out in the privacy of her music
room, where the two express their love for each other.

He has found her with her nun's bonnet removed and draws from
her the confession that she wears it, not because of a promise to the
Virgin Mary, but at the advice of Father Benicio, who had offered
this solution, rather than suicide or divorce, to keep her husband
away from her. The union of Strawbridge and another man's wife is
partly a physiological response which, Stribling makes it appear, occurs outside the pale of moral judgment and is partly justified by
their mutual love. In this sense, the behavior of Strawbridge and
Dolores Fombombo resembles that of other love partners in
Stribling's novels, of which Abner Teeftallow and Nessie Sutton in
*Teeftallow*, Agatha Pomeroy and Risdale Balus in *Bright Metal*, and
Caridius and Mary Littenham in *The Sound Wagon* are examples.

After this experience with Dolores, Strawbridge begins making
plans for their escape together — ironically, at just the moment that
the general chooses to honor Strawbridge publicly with a medal for
his bravery during the attack on San Geronimo. With surprise and
dismay, Strawbridge learns that both his love and his plan for escape
are known to many of the city's populace. His plans are foiled,
however, by the priest who once enjoyed a stolen horse but cannot
now sanction a stolen wife. To the unhappy Dolores, Father Benicio
preaches renunciation, warning her that the present anguish is

nothing in comparison with the "fires of remorse" that would burn in her heart should she leave her husband. Even Strawbridge succumbs temporarily to the arguments of the priest and almost accepts the idea that "if you take away from Dolores the holy sacraments which support her life, you can never have one unsullied caress from the woman you adore" (238). As the lovers part, Stribling focuses attention on the picture of the Last Supper hanging in the chapel.

When Strawbridge moves into the church to await his departure from the country and to avoid frequent contact with Dolores in the palace, the priest almost brings him to repentance for his sins. But Strawbridge eventually sees that a sin is a mistake which causes pain, that "the only difference between the repentance of a saint and the chagrin of a cutpurse caught in the toil of the law, is the class of mistakes in their lives which brings them pain, and from which, in spirit, they turn" (251). The father and the gun salesman realize pain on far different levels. Also the father is not above the use of prevarication to gain his own ends. When he tells Strawbridge that Dolores has entered a convent, the American believes him; but he later discovers from an old crone how foolish he has been when she shouts, "You believed a priest in a case like that!" (267).

The sacking of Canelejos; the murder of Fombombo by thousands of dirty, starved, escaped prisoners under Saturnino's direction; and the rejoicing over the new dictator, Lubito, leave Strawbridge nauseated. Particularly revolting is the revelation of his own part in these anarchic events. Locating Dolores, he makes a dramatic escape down the river with her. On the way, he receives a message from Lubito offering to buy guns and advising him that all of the officials and sympathizers of the former government have been placed in prison. "Be assured," the message says, "that none of them will ever get out, except in sacks. I am determined that in Rio Negro shall reign liberty, equality, and fraternity. I have also recaptured a large number of 'reds' [Communists] and have set them to digging the foundation of a magnificent bull-ring" (311).

The characters presented by Stribling in *Fombombo* typically act in defiance of their own stated principles and never realize that the statement and the action are at variance. Stribling's protagonists are average people who are caught in the same web with all the other characters of his fictional world. Accepting things as they are, with all our definitions and identifications properly in mind, we can ask, Why should a man who recognizes the folly of revolution sell guns and ammunition to revolutionists? How can a priest justify the telling of a lie? How can a genteel religious young wife give herself to a brash, uncouth salesman? How can an intelligent newspaper editor talk about liberty in the presence of innocent prisoners? When faced with such questions as these, Stribling seems to be saying that, in certain moments in the lives of men, the only course of action morally possible lies along immoral lines. But the recognition of appearance for appearance's sake requires a superman, and the closest a human being can come to such recognition is some feeling of remorse or a twinge of conscience. And this recognition, as seen in Strawbridge's experience, can be readily rationalized into nonexistence.

Stribling paints his characters — and his thesis — in broad strokes. Every detail, including the examples of poetry, points to the same conclusion. The selections of poetry, attributed to one or another "great" American poet, are notably and purposefully bad; and Stribling has Strawbridge call them great only to emphasize his lack of culture. He is the product of a nation without a cultural heritage, whose only yardstick of success is marked in dollars. Strawbridge has nothing of refinement about him; his personality — like his business suit — is designed to please the customer.

As far as Strawbridge can determine, Venezuela needs his advice (or any good American's advice) to improve its economy; but his philosophy is based on the idea that anything new is an improvement. He cannot fathom the idea that anything old might have merit, nor can he accept the possibility that time culls the trivial from the mediocre. The Latins, on the other hand, cannot imagine a new present. Clinging to the past, they believe that, just as examples of superior music multiply with the passing years, so too will examples of men like Simon Bolivar. And their heroic deeds, like great symphonies, will live on forever. Strawbridge's indignation in finding Bolivar compared with George Washington is part of the pattern of his thinking. For him, the event produced the man, just as a flaw in an old mechanism leads to the production of a new model. That any United States general should try to become another George Washington never occurs to him. But the Latins look always for another Simon Bolivar, and they are totally unaware that the conditions which made Bolivar a hero no longer exist. In the end, Lubito should be the new man for the new age, but he is not. He has followed the pattern of the old dictators, and his demise will be like theirs. Thus, in the sense that Latin sentimentality has failed again and that the new leader is doomed not to succeed, American materialism may be said to triumph. But the dilemma is not resolved, for the sentimentality still flourishes — and Strawbridge plans to marry Senora Fombombo.

The Senora represents what Americans do not have — old-world customs and an old-world treasury of fine music and great literature. She has genteel manners and a firm faith in God. When Strawbridge thinks of her, he thinks of a long convenant of grandchildren and great-grandchildren; in her, the heritage of life and art are one. This concept is far different from Strawbridge's previous one of babies as the "absurd accidents of dual living" rather than as the end of matrimony.

Consistent with his objective stance, Stribling in *Fombombo*, as in his other novels, does not attempt to force an opinion on the reader. He neither criticizes nor moralizes; he merely shows that Strawbridge is a product of materialistic society, one whose members feel they have an inalienable right to the pursuit of property. To Strawbridge, the benefits of increased capital accrue to the nation as a whole. Stribling does not state that all Americans are ignorant of cultural values, but he implies that their desire for material equality leads economically lower- and middle-class individuals to pursue money to such an extent that only after the accumulation of wealth can they begin to acquire culture. Thus, in both the United States and Venezuela, a member of what we might lightly term the nouveau riche finds himself not only adjusting to, but also competing with, elements he had not foreseen. Without the proper background, he cannot successfully compete; the background cannot be acquired so easily or so quickly as money, and thus he inevitably fails. Strawbridge is one of these persons — a member of the vast middle class, which is above poverty and below culture.

Unable to foresee all these problems, Strawbridge has a necessarily limited vision. Nevertheless, in Senora Dolores, he senses a desirable quality, intangible, but having value — a quality which transcends the present and, as in the instance of his thoughts on the grandchildren, endows the future with some additional significance. Exactly what the significance might be, he has not at the end of the novel had time or opportunity to discern. But, if Cissie Dildine is to be an agent of Peter Siner's learning in *Birthright*, so too is Senora Dolores to be an agent of Strawbridge's education in *Fombombo*. Perhaps a second generation of Siners will succeed in utilizing their education, and perhaps a second generation of Strawbridges will succeed in possessing both money and culture.

## II  *From Sun to Shade*

*Red Sand,* the second of the Venezuelan novels, differs from the
first one in its simplicity of theme. It has in it no Strawbridge to express criticism and no Gumersindo to reply. Rather than two
spokesmen of conflicting views, Stribling presents only a Latin
protagonist, just as he is and not as an American thinks he should be.
Angelito, a mixture of conflicts, differs from Strawbridge, who was
unaware of the discrepancy between what he was and what he
thought he was. Angelito knows what he is — a peon, and what he
wants to be — a member of the aristocracy. For him, the bullring, instead of art or letters or money or education, will provide the opening wedge into the ranks of the aristocracy.

As *Fombombo* shows, there is no middle class in Venezuela, in
that the merchant class remains notably poor, and the distinctions
between poor and rich are clearly drawn. Apparently in all of
Caracas, Angelito is the only person ambitious and optimistic
enough to attempt to cross those lines. At the beginning of the novel,
he is already a successful torero and owns a large blue casa from
which one may look down upon the city. Dominating the view,
however, is a large circular mass — the bullring, on the side of which
appears the inscription *Sol y Sombra;* and, because the sun is
malevolent, the wealthy sit in the shade. Since bullfighting may be
viewed as a type of suicide, Angelito's passage from sun into shade
corresponds with the events of his life.

To complicate his rise in society, Angelito's mother insists upon
playing the role of the peasant woman she is; she is too old to change
— and any attempt to change is regarded by her as the result of a
feeling of guilt. True to herself, and much to her son's embarrass-
ment, she continues to dress as a peasant woman; to haggle over
pennies in the poor markets; and, most humiliating of all, to sell
lottery tickets. Outside the blue casa, the fountain is dry, and guavas
grow in the garden. For Ana, poverty is a way of life; and water,
along with all that it symbolizes, is illustrative of wealth and is not to
be desired by one of her class. Inside the blue casa, she inhabits the
servant's quarters, where she is the only servant. Here she becomes
involved in a distasteful duplicity: she is Angelito's mother when
they are alone, but she is his servant when anyone else is around.
Her grumbling discontentment with Angelito's ambition does not
prevent her, however, from switching roles with an amazing alacrity,
nor does it diminish her pleasure in the distinguished company her
son sometimes keeps.

At the other end of the class spectrum is Rafael Jiminez, a member of the aristocracy, who wants to be a bullfighter and a writer of poetry. His position, his ambitions, and, consequently, his meditations make of him a spokesman for a new age. Where democracy, or a crossing of old social barriers, or a lifting of social restrictions is apparent, he, because of his humanitarian ideals, is responsible. Unhappy with his fiancée, he continues to live with the unhappiness, explaining that "every person's idea of happiness is a bundle of contradictions. To acquire one thing, a person must sacrifice some other thing. The more you think about it the simpler it grows and . . . the more absurd."[2]

The truth of Rafael's statement is revealed in every aspect of Angelito's own life. The most devastating example occurs when, to acquire Rafael's sister for a wife, he must fight a duel with her original fiancé, the aristocratic and wealthy newspaper publisher, Senor Montauban. In the duel, Angelito brings disgrace upon himself by losing his temper and his self-control and by using the peon's unethical fighting techniques. Rafael explains the incident by pointing out that only confusion and dishonor can come from a mixing of the classes, particularly in anything so formal as a duel. That Angelito is aware, in his own peasant way, of the same principle, is evidenced by an earlier conversation with his mother in which he tries to explain why his "friends" would want to see him risk his life every Sunday: "Aristocratic friends are not like peon friends. Peons fall in with each other anyway, rich or poor, clad or naked, full or hungry they are always the same. But friendship among aristocrats is more like a game. One must be prepared to play, or Ca! one can't play! Aristocrats have standards, something to live up to, a fine casa, honor, bravery, money. If you fail to have these, out you go among the peons. That is fair. Friendship among the aristocrats is a game like a bullfight" (76).

Angelito understands intellectually the importance of remaining faithful to standards of conduct, but he forgets emotionally. But even his intellectual understanding is limited. He does not realize that faithfulness to standards is a matter of breeding, a code instilled practically from the day of birth. In this sense, although he strives to develop that kind of faithfulness, he can never become an aristocrat because there will always be instances, as in the ill-fated duel, when he reverts to type.

Angelito, in contemplating his chosen agent for social advancement, thinks it strange that he should bring pleasure to thousands of people by risking his life in fighting bulls. Speaking through another character, Stribling points out that bullfighting, like war, can be a kind of purification for a nation. Unlike war, however, it does not involve too great a sacrifice of life and wealth. The bull "represents the prodigious forces of nature, vast, furious, and brutal"; and, because "the national sport of the Spanish people is the sincere battle to death between a bull and a man, the whole Spanish race finds itself more at home in the world than do less favored nations" (120). Later, just before Angelito's last great exhibition, Stribling explains that the bullfight is art — a presentation of life that is "pregnant with the austere and beautiful truth that the fitting end of life is death, that the feverish round of our days is held in the bosom of eternity. It eases the petty raptures and anguish of its own spectacle against the dark infinitude of nothingness" (284).

Angelito cannot understand the bullfight as art; and, unlike Juan Leon, a torero from the ranks of the aristocracy, he cannot reach the level of artistry in his efforts in the arena. Juan Leon can make of the bullfight an art, because he has refinement and skill and because he works with the best tools — the purebred Spanish fighting bulls he brings with him. Because he is an aristocrat, he can be different with aplomb; he does not, as the fashion dictates, call himself "Leonito," and he chooses to wear a black fighting regalia. In the ring, Angelito watches while Juan, with superb technique, subordinates himself to "exhibit the grace, the speed, the strength and monumental lines of the bull" (307); and, following Stribling's description, we might indeed ask, How can we tell the dancer from the dance? In Juan Leon, art and life are one: "The drama passed beyond the bounds of an event in flesh and blood. It breathed an immortal beauty. This charging bull was one with the Discobulus or the group of Laocoon. With the solidity of a statue it blended the color of a painting and the movement and suspense of drama" (308).

Against this kind of competition, Angelito has not a chance to break into the ranks of the aristocracy. Opposite Juan Leon, Angelito is a blasphemer, since his is a performance of skill without art; but, as he enters the ring after Juan, he is still trying. This time, in fact, he is more motivated to try harder: Socorro Jiminez agrees to become his bride, and Angelito must prove that he deserves a place in her family. In this, his last bullfight, he engages in a series of juggling tricks that bring wild applause from the poor "sol" side of the arena; but his object and his great need is to use this performance to cut across class lines. He succeeds, finally, not through refinement and skill, but through pure daring which peonizes "even the critical taste of 'sombra.' He had bludgeoned them into a crude primitive worship of rashness and peril; he had effaced the cool aristocratic universe of ideal beauty. He had won" (319). Angelito in this exhibition again reverts to type; as in the critical duel with Montauban, when Angelito needs additional strength, it has to come from the inherent nature of the peon. No amount of money, no number of aristocratic associations that are merely a veneer, can provide for him the strength that he needs. Ironically, at the moment of triumph, a pain from the wound he received in the duel with Montauban flares and causes him a momentary loss of precision. His entire career is telescoped into a few moments as he is tossed on the horns of the bull: "The amphitheater seemed to swing up and down, into the sunshine, into the shadow, the sunshine, the shadow" (320). The agent of Angelito's success has proved the agent of his destruction.

When Angelito remarked earlier in the novel that the aristocrats "are faithful to their standards: honor, bravery, power," he spoke better than he knew. When at his death he no longer holds his place with his rapier, they exclude him, as he had predicted, from their society. Socorro is deemed too ill to attend his funeral, and the rest of the family would rather forget the unfortunate engagement. Only his mother and Rafael attend to mourn him. The former, in keeping with the peon custom, has rented a temporary vault for his body; after a time, his bones will be cast over the hill. Even in death, Angelito does not succeed in entering the society of the rich. His only triumph, in Rafael's judgment, is that he had provided for Socorro a brief glimpse of real love; because of him, Socorro had lived.

*Red Sand* is without question Angelito's book, and he looms large in it. Possessed of pride and hope, he struggles against fate; but, like so many greater literary creations than he, he fails — his flaw, an overconsciousness of an unfortunate background. But, as a product of an environment which he cannot escape, Angelito is the character through whom Stribling explores the nature of Venezuela's "age-long wounds." Because of the suppression of the masses, the wounds themselves are, symbolically, mistakes made in the name of freedom and justice. These wounds, moreover, cripple even more a people who, under Bolivar, had gained some slight victory in overthrowing the Spanish monarchs. The wounds are "age-long," because the same evils which inflicted them on the masses continue to flourish.

In *Fombombo*, Stribling treats the nature of Latin political instability. The dictator sees that the peon never understands what has kept him in a subjective position; and he perceives that, as long as the peons occupy it, they are ripe for exploitation by any revolutionary who will provide them with arms and thereby give them new power, making of them possible terrorists. For his part, the peon, with no middle class open to him, is vaguely aware that there is no means of improving his lot. Thus, he invariably yields to the oratory of the would-be dictator and takes up arms to gain for himself not merely an improvement in his position but a direct access to the position of the rich. Stribling leaves Lubito temporarily holding sway in Orinoco province and, in *Red Sand*, turns to Angelito in Caracas. Having gained a knowledge of the bulls by working in a slaughterhouse, Angelito attempts to challenge the social structure. This structure he finds is more permanent and at the same time more elusive than political standing. A gun cannot destroy it, nor is there in the social world anything so easily attainable as a gun to endow the usurper with strength. The sociopolitical structure is at fault, and any means which attacks only one element of the twofold system is doomed to failure. If the lot of the poor is to be improved, another, all-inclusive, means must be found; and this process must be one of education, not merely of acquisition of property. To summarize, in *Fombombo*, the would-be dictators use politics and force in an attempt to leap the chasm between the lower and upper classes; in *Red Sand*, Angelito attempts the same leap through his prowess in the bullring; but neither succeeds in breaking into the ranks of the aristocracy.

Both *Fombombo* and *Red Sand* are good illustrations of Stribling's ability to use melodramatic plots as vehicles for social criticism. Neither novel has the impact on the reader that *Birthright* has, probably because Stribling was a too-far-removed observer of the Venezuelan scene. At the same time, however, *Fombombo* and *Red Sand* are testaments to his acute powers of observation and his skill in ordering what he observes into cohesive fictional structures that keep the reader interested. Moreover, these Venezuelan novels represent a forward step in Stribling's artistic development, in that they reflect a judicious blending of humor, irony, and pathos. While Stribling may not have considered these works to be serious fictional efforts, they nevertheless stand on their own as quality novels and as examples of the novelist's versatility.

## CHAPTER 4

# Diogenes in Tennessee

THE small town has always had an important place in America's national mythology — being veiwed more often than not as a last bastion of democracy, friendship, and happiness. Although the standardization of culture engendered by modern industrialization and urbanization has brought about the decline of the small town in fact, it has done little to diminish the image of the small town in myth. While the rest of the world has perhaps been spinning on its way to perdition, the small town has remained a symbol for all that is good and decent. This myth Stribling exposes in *Teeftallow*, a novel published in 1926.

*Teeftallow*, set in the hill country of Tennessee, is basically the story of Abner Teeftallow, a simple, colorless, rustic lad of eighteen who has been reared on the Lane County poor farm. Although in one sense, the novel deals with Abner's maturing, it is not a novel of initiation; for the boy undergoes no real spiritual change. Indeed, what happens to him in the novel may be summarized rather quickly. Working as a railroad construction hand, he gets Nessie Sutton, a hill girl, pregnant and leaves her; he finds himself wealthy because of land grants inherited from his grandfather; he has an unconsummated love affair with Adelaide Jones, the daughter of a scheming speculator; he loses his land grants in a swindle; and he finally returns to Nessie and his newborn daughter. Abner, then, is not the most significant of protagonists and, moreover, is not a direct participant in many of the incidents in the novel — which themselves do not move in any consistent or sequential pattern to a culmination of the action. Rather, they follow one another in an episodic structure that enables Stribling to focus upon various aspects of life in the Tennessee hill country and on the various characters involved.

45

## I  *Comin' to the Front Shore*

"Just another stride forward in our county's progress. Ever'thing's
getting better. That railroad will give an outlet for our products;
bring trade and travel our way. Old Lane's comin' to the front
shore!"[1] These are the thoughts of James Sandage, overseer of the
Lane County poor farm, as he drives his jalopy over the rutted roads
of the area. Such thoughts are strikingly reminiscent of Sinclair
Lewis's George Babbitt and his views of Zenith. James Sandage,
however, is not really the booster type; and none of the villages of
Lane County can boast any towers, like those of Zenith, that aspire
"above the morning mist; austere towers of steel and cement and
limestone, sturdy as cliffs and delicate as silver rods."[2]

On the contrary, Lane County is a rather dreary and monotonous
place. Like so many areas of the South, it was isolated during the
period between the Civil War and the 1920s from the main stream of
the nation's economic and social development. Its villages are not
the quaint hamlets of the American myth of the small town; they are
shabby and dirty. Nor are its inhabitants the friendly, hard-working
people who populate the mythical small town; they are bigoted, ignorant, and crude; they are prone to violent actions; they are strong
in their fear of God but weak in their personal morality; they distrust
anything legal and admire anyone who can "put one over" on the
law. Old Lane may be coming to the "front shore" economically,
but socially it is still a backward and frightfully narrow community
with a fundamental, tenacious belief in God and the Bible, a belief
well-illustrated in a stanza of its favorite revival hymn —

> Holy Bi-yi-bul, blessed Bi-yi-bul,
> Gift of God, and the lamp of life,
> Beautiful Bibul thou art mine.
> I cling to the dear old Holy Bi-yi-bul —

or in the titles of the sermons preached at its revival meetings: "The
Dance of Evil, or Foxtrotting to Hell"; "Evolution, or From College
to Damnation"; "Novel Reading, or From Print to Perdition";
"Scarlet Women and Dingy Men" (for men only); "Bobbed Hair
and Bobbed Morals" (for women only). Against this background,
Stribling places Abner Teeftallow and the assortment of characters
around him.

Abner's hero, and the man responsible for the railroad that is com-

ing to Lane County, is Railroad Jones, a clever, unscrupulous financial promoter, who, though he can neither read nor write, has an un-
canny memory. One of the best-drawn characters in the novel, he is
an example of the American frontier rogue of the Simon Suggs tradition. If Suggs's motto was "It's good to be shifty in a new country,"
Jones's motto is "It's good to be shifty in any country." His schemes
give the hill people a sense of pleasure, especially when they are
directed at "city smart-alecks," thus satisfying the hill man's vague
feeling of animosity toward the great world beyond the hills. The hill
people, not trusting the law of the outside world, see a certain ironic
justice in beating the enemy with his own weapons.

The leading citizen in Irontown, the community where the story
opens, is Perry Northcutt, the banker. Two things occupy his mind,
his bank and his religion; and he is as adept at keeping these two interests in their respective niches in his life as Railroad Jones is at
keeping his conscience from dulling his business acumen. On the
day that the construction workers receive their wages, Northcutt
stands behind the teller's window in his bank and verbally browbeats
the ignorant hill men into depositing a considerable portion of their
money. Only when he is threatened with bodily harm does he relent
and give a worker his full pay. He is in many respects like Henry
Hooker, the banker in *Birthright,* in that he can turn from money
grubbing at the bank to soul saving at the church.

To Perry Northcutt, people from the South stand just a little closer
to God than do any others; and his own position, as he sees it, is at
the head of the line. The first glimpse we have of brother Perry's acting in the name of religion is on the Sunday that Ditmas, a construction engineer for the railroad and a northern agnostic, schedules a
baseball game for the workers. Urged on by his fire-eating and
Bible-quoting sister, Northcutt attempts to stop such desecration of
the Sabbath. Dressed in funereal black, he approaches the ball field
with a conciliatory smile and, speaking as if to children, scolds the
workers for even thinking of desecrating the Sabbath by playing
ball. But, retiring to their closets and seeking the Lord in prayer,
does not seem a suitable substitute for a ball game to Perry's
audience. One voice points out that Saturday and not Sunday is
really the Sabbath — to which Northcutt shouts angrily, "Look
here . . . when Christ came to this earth, you know the old dispensa-
tion was finished and a new one began. They changed the day of
worship from Saturday to Sunday" (76).

The workers finally disperse; but, before they do, A. M. Belshue, a local jeweler and a nonbeliever, confronts Northcutt with the question of what makes him believe there is a God. The exchange that follows is similar to that between William Jennings Bryan and Clarence Darrow in the Dayton, Tennessee, monkey trial.[3] Northcutt, who refuses to be baited into an argument with "any infidel," states that he does not have to prove the existence of God because he *knows* that God exists. "Once I was prayin' to Him when my little daughter died," says brother Perry, "and He came down and touched my head and blessed me. Praise His holy name! Praise God! He brought me a peace you will never know, Andy Belshue, till you find God, too" (78). To Belshue's retort that such a visitation from God was merely the product of imagination, Northcutt cries, "My imagination! Don't you think I know my own Father's voice" (78).

It is not strange, then, that Perry Northcutt is convinced that Irontown is in dire need of a revival; and he urges that the event be soon because of an excess of drinking, gambling, and cursing. He sends a plea for help to the Reverend Blackman, "the Big Bertha of Heaven," who is famous for clearing out bootleggers and gamblers and for generally "blasting hell" out of a town.

Stribling presents an excellent picture of the protracted meeting that the Reverend Blackman conducts in Irontown. A typical hill-country revival with all the flavor of the frontier, it is punctuated with singing, shouting, clapping, and sobbing; and the preacher exhorts all to desist from following the devil and to "Come to Je-e-e-sus! Come to Je-e-e-sus! He will sa-a-ave you! He will sa-a-ave you!" (153). Everyday life in Irontown may be humdrum, but excitement runs high during a protracted revival meeting. Perry Northcutt, for example, who does not drink, smoke, or curse, and whose wife is fat and obstinate, "compressed his whole emotional outlet into an annual protracted meeting" (139), praying incessantly and fasting for two whole days. At the end of the second day, while praying in his home, "he felt God stroke his thin hair and say, 'My son, your faith shall be rewarded by the greatest revival Irontown has ever known'" (139).

The irony in such a protracted meeting, of course, is that the very evils that people like Northcutt wish to stamp out provide the emotional outlets for the less "godly" inhabitants of Irontown in the same way that religion does for the "soldiers of the Lord." Abner, for example, finds "profound relief" and "spiritual refreshment" in the succession of suspenses and denouements of a crap game. As the game goes on, and Abner's pile of money alternately grows and shrinks, his attention is "focused on the shooting with cataleptic intensity" and the blood pounds in his temples. When the play is stopped momentarily because of a misunderstanding, he feels a sense of exasperation as he crouches over his money waiting for the game to resume. When it does, "it seemed as if some intolerable gap had been bridged. Abner's nerves settled in their cycle of suspense, denouement, pleasure, pain. He made his hazard concerning the future, even if that future were separated from the present by the merest tick of time. Still he was using his powers of forecasting, a functioning his daily life did not hold. The stars of the summer night wove slowly overhead as these devotees of the dark Goddess of Chance knelt at their devotions" (69).

Here, then, is another brand of Irontown religion; and its ritual and jargon are just as specialized as that in the local Methodist Church. Moreover, the sanctions that it places upon its followers are just as strict. A Negro who tries to use loaded dice is thrown bodily out of the circle of crap shooters and is lucky to get off so easily. In the primitive game of craps, punishment is just and swift; there is no hypocrisy. Civilized Irontown's punishment, however, may be quite unjust, and considerable hypocrisy exists.

Two graphic examples of the hypocrisy in Irontown Christianity stand out in the book. The first stems from an incident in which Peck Bradley, the village no-good, shoots Tug Beavers. Tug himself is hardly one of Irontown's model citizens, but his wounding awakens swift and almost diametrically opposed reactions. The first grows out of Peck's flight. The upholders of Irontown justice immediately set out with bloodhounds to run him down and eventually succeed. The progress of the chase is eagerly followed by the community, first through on-the-spot reporters, then through telephone calls, and finally through rumor. Meanwhile, Mrs. Roxie Biggers, Perry Northcutt's sister, visits Tug's rooming house, where he is recovering from his wound, and becomes a kind of one-woman committee for the welfare of Tug Beavers. Mrs. Biggers never "gave anything to charity herself except her services, but these services were dynamic" (164). This is the other reaction in Irontown. Perhaps we can call it compassion; but, at the same time, Mrs. Biggers feels only hatred for Peck Bradley and is the instigator of the plot to lynch him. The plot succeeds, and Peck is lynched. As Abner comes upon the scene just after the lynching, he sees a slowly swinging body that has been grossly mutilated by souvenir hunters and feels a terrible sense of insecurity that a human being could be so quickly and grotesquely "focused to pure intellect."

The lynching of Peck Bradley is considered an "unqualified moral triumph in Irontown, and out of the sweet oil of the lynching flowered other blossoms of practical morality" (191). Bootleggers, gamblers, prostitutes — all are waited on by delegations of Irontown citizens bent on making their village a moral example for the world. Abner, who feels at first some sympathy for these offenders of morality, is soon sucked in by the excitement. Although he cannot see the right in drinking a man's liquor or in enjoying a woman's favors and then in the next moment running them out of town, he is not able to extend his point of view. Thus, the men of the town self-righteously drive out the "undesirables" — and we have the second major example of Irontown hypocrisy.

## II  *Some Chinks in the Wall*

In the second book of *Teeftallow*, the focus is no longer on the religious aspect of the hill village but on the economic forces that industrialization brings. The scene is shifted a few miles from Irontown to Lanesburg, the county seat; Abner assumes a more significant role in the events; and we have the reentrance of Railroad Jones, along with his daughter Adelaide, who does not appear in the first book at all. James Sandage is again the first person we see; and he, in a sense, has come to "the front shore," along with Lane County. As a result of the railroad, he has become a part of the trend toward materialism, rising from his position at the poor farm to county trustee and private investor. His success leads to his fall, however, because he has been investing county funds with Railroad Jones. When Jones does not pay back the money, Sandage goes to jail. Jones has a scheme to make everything come out all right for both Sandage and himself; but Sandage, who has not become completely corrupt, refuses to compromise additionally the trust put in him by the voters. Jones's answer to Sandage is that people really admire those who can beat them out of public funds and would do the same thing themselves if they only knew how.

Railroad Jones is a man who has made an evaluation of the world he lives in and who has made his choices accordingly. He is "Babtis' enough to b'lieve that what is to be will be; an' sence it shore is goin' to happen, my plan is to hit fust an' make it happen to the other feller" (306). Some people, like Sandage perhaps, may find themselves caught in a moral dilemma between Christian and business ethics, but not Jones. Just as Perry Northcutt can compartmentalize religion and business, Jones can remove religion as a force almost completely from his life. After he cheats Ditmas in a land transaction, he justifies it to Abner on the basis that, in trading, the universal rule is that every man must look out for himself.

Ditmas, in a state of inebriation after being swindled, has a clear insight into the legal ways of the South and of the entire country. Through Ditmas's drunken remarks, Stribling touches on the theme that he develops more fully later in the trilogy — that of the decline of the spiritual in favor of the material. This theme, however, is treated not morally but ironically, and the only response that Ditmas's comments elicit from Abner is, "He shore is drunk" (286).

Abner, at this point, is unable to grasp any significance in such views as Ditmas holds; for as a product of his environment, Abner lacks the understanding that would enable him to achieve a wider vision. In this sense, he is representative of all the inhabitants of Lane County. Even when he finds himself rich through land claims held by his grandfather, his reaction is stoically unimaginative; and, like all hill people, according to Stribling, he relishes the prospect of a completely idle life.

Abner sees his new position of wealth in a strictly mechanistic way — a result of sheer chance. When Shallburger, the labor organizer, tries to persuade him to use his influence on the labor side, Abner calls him a fool and exclaims, "Let the rich man stand by the rich an' the pore by the pore! Now, by God, I'm rich an' I'm standin' with 'em, an' if you don't like it you can go to hell!" (328 - 29). When Shallburger resorts to the concepts of right, justice, and charity, Abner retaliates with a biblical defense of "skin 'em when you can, an' that's in the Bible, Shallburger, an' there's no gittin' around that!" (329). To Shallburger's argument that the Bible knows nothing of modern-day social and labor problems, Abner solemnly interposes, "When you butt yore head agin the Bible you'r buttin agin a stone wall" (329).

There are, however, a couple of chinks in the stone wall that the hill people have fashioned around themselves out of the Bible. The first one, obviously, is industrialization with its concomitant social problems. The socialistic philosophy that Shallburger holds is antithetical to the entire background of the hill man; to him, "It's a plan to divide up all the work into such little bits, everybody will be out of a job most of the time" (124). Moreover, socialism is a negation of the frontier spirit of individualism and distrust of government that has been bred in him. Though the problem is not solved in *Teef-tallow*, Stribling leaves us with the feeling that it eventually will force considerable change in the tenor of life in Lane County.

The other chink comes through education and some contact with life beyond the hill country. Adelaide Jones has been away to school, and her somewhat liberated views are in stark contrast with those of tradition-bound Lane County. Her influence on Abner, for example, is significant in that through her the hill boy is exposed to a completely new view of life. Adelaide is willing to experiment with sex: to her, hugging and kissing serve as a tryout for passion; and petting parties, while they cause complaints from more conservative quarters, save hundreds from divorces. Adelaide is of a new generation, and she accepts sex and love as vital components in the life process, something that the hill people have never done — at least not openly.

Abner thinks he loves Adelaide, but she rejects him. From here on, the novel draws rapidly to a close. Abner sees Nessie again and the little daughter she has borne him. He is legally cheated out of his land holdings by Railroad Jones, who in turn is burned to death in his office by James Sandage. To leave the path clear for Abner and Nessie to get back together, Stribling has Belshue, who had earlier married Nessie when Abner left her, commit suicide by walking into the path of a train. All of this action is a bit contrived, but it does not cloud the basic impression that we are left with at the end. Abner, as we have noted, is not changed essentially in the course of the novel. At the end, he is still a colorless and unimaginative rustic — and Nessie is still a hill girl.

The experiences that these two young people have had, however, have given them glimpses of emotional and spiritual freedom; and as Abner, remembering the "curl of a little rose-leaf baby's palm around his thumb," sets his face "against the wintry rock-bound hill" (405) and starts toward Nessie's house, we are left with much the same impression that we are at the end of *Birthright*. Like Peter and Cissie, Abner and Nessie are a part of a slow evolutionary process. Whatever hope exists for the future of Lane County must, in the final analysis, lie with its own.

### III   *A Level of Reality*

Exploiting various character types — the ignorant hill girl, the unscrupulous and clever speculator, the fundamentalist pillar of society, the northern agnostic, etc. — Stribling in *Teeftallow* blends storytelling with social criticism in a penetrating study of the hill-country mind. In this sense, the novel brings out what Stribling felt to be a significant level of life in the Tennessee hill country. What happens in *Teeftallow* could not happen anywhere but in the Tennessee hills, or at least in some similar setting. The atmosphere of Irontown, for example, makes a definite impression on the mind of the reader at the same time that it has a definite impact upon the characters. Here, Abner Teeftallow, unobtrusive protagonist that he is, stands as a most notable illustration. As witness to, or participant in, many of the novel's episodes, he reflects the narrowness of vision emanating from the background out of which he comes. He is, moreover, an unconscious victim of this vision, as are so many of the other characters in the novel.

Some readers may wish that Stribling had made Abner into a protagonist with whom they could more easily identify, but character development or motivation is not what the novelist was interested in when he wrote *Teeftallow*. He was more interested in examining hill-country mores with the eye of a reporter and in recording what he saw. From that standpoint, *Teeftallow* deserves a distinct niche in the realm of realistic writing.

CHAPTER 5

# More Views of the Hill Country

THE years 1928 through 1930 were busy and productive ones for Tom Stribling. He published three novels — *Bright Metal* (1928); *Strange Moon* (1929); and *Backwater* (1930) — and a book of mystery stories, *Clues of the Carribees* (1929). In *Strange Moon* and *Clues of the Carribees*, Stribling turned once again to Latin America for a setting. The novel is the story of Eugene Manners, an American oil man who finds love and adventure in Venezuela. A tour de force, the novel moves swiftly and suspensefully, and it presents considerable Venezuelan local color. There are good pictures of the status of peons and of the views of aristocrats as contrasted with American business ethics. *Clues of the Carribees* contains five stories, each featuring Henry Poggioli, a professor of psychology at Ohio State University who is on leave in the Carribees. He turns detective and, through astute putting together of strange and varied clues, solves several complicated mysteries. *Bright Metal* and *Backwater* both deal with the South and, for the purposes of this study, have the most significance. Of these two, *Bright Metal* is by far the better novel.

## I  An Early Version of Women's Liberation

Abner Teeftallow, as we have seen, had no preconceived ideals or beliefs; but the same observation cannot be made about newly married Agatha Pomeroy, the protagonist of *Bright Metal*. A New Yorker removed to the South, Agatha is not a Carol Kennicutt in the full sense, but she is not much different from Sinclair Lewis's heroine in *Main Street*. Agatha does not wish to influence her Tennessee hill town and make it beautiful, as Carol would like to do with a prairie town; but she cannot reconcile herself to the pettiness and narrowness that she finds in and around Lanesburg, Tennessee.

54

She does not have Carol's lofty ideals about banishing ugliness and provincialism from a given locale; but, at the same time, she is not the kind of woman who sits idly by and lets the status quo go undisturbed.

*Bright Metal* has two plots, each a part of the other — Agatha's efforts toward making the women of Lane County an important force in politics and her relationship with Risdale Balus, a young hill man with whom she feels a great affinity. By having Agatha become involved in politics, Stribling provides himself the opportunity for realistically and satirically examining this area of hill life — an area "in which a knight errant might travel as far as he liked in any direction and find plenty of wrongs to right."[1] By bringing Risdale into the novel, Stribling is able to emphasize his idea of sex as a vital component in the evolution of life. Taken together, these two plots contain the theme of the novel — Agatha's counter-education in the hill country and the conflict within herself that it engenders.

Agatha's stereotyped image of the South as a land of graceful mansions inhabited by dashing men and beautiful women does not hold up in the face of reality. The first change that she is forced to make in her idealized image of the South comes when her husband, Calhoun Pomeroy (Pom), tells her that there are no magnolia trees in Tennessee. She also soon becomes aware that at least not all of the South is a colorful region of beautiful mansions. As the bridal couple drives farther south, the well-kept farm houses of the North give way to neglected and weatherworn buildings, and the very farms themselves present a disorganized array of deserted fields given over to weeds and occasional patches of corn ripening amid stumps and dead trees. The whole scene presents an image of desolation and near sterility and, as such, reflects the kind of society that it sustains.

The road that the Pomeroys drive on, however, is new and looks out of place amid its surroundings. Like Railroad Jones's railroad in *Teeftallow*, the road is a mark of progress in the efforts of civilization (and the government) to draw the Tennessee hill country into its sphere. Its route, however, does not follow a logical pattern from town to town; it runs through land owned by wealthy and politically influential men, thus boosting the prices of their land. Once again, Stribling wastes little time in establishing the targets of his criticism. Indeed, before Agatha can reach her new home, she comes into contact with another aspect of the South for which she is not prepared — the local constable. Fatty Bobbs (whom we met in *Birthright*) is another who enforces the law in his own fashion — one that more

often than not benefits him or his friends. As in *Birthright*, Stribling
depicts him more as an instrument of injustice than of justice.

The Pomeroy family, with whom the newlyweds are to live, is
made up of old Mother Pomeroy and Pom's sister Parilee. The
mother is as tradition bound, both religiously and socially, as any hill
woman. Parilee is a schoolteacher who, though almost as narrow as
her mother, shows occasional signs of seeing through the iron curtain
of tradition. But she is unable to do more than see. There is
something vaguely feminine about her room, but the bleakness of it
dominates. The dried-up chrysanthemum and the iron bedstead
with a pink cover "somehow bespoke the anchorite in whom sex had
dwindled to a faint decorative impulse without further connotations" (42).

Parilee's logic regarding the Tennessee legislature's requirement
that she take a correspondence course in biology to retain her
teaching certificate illustrates her inability to break the bonds of
tradition. She objects to the course because it teaches evolution, a
concept which Tennessee law forbids and which, to Parilee,the Bible
also forbids. To her, the law forbiding the teaching of evolution
is a step in raising educational standards in Tennessee; and she cannot understand why the legislature should in the next breath force
Christian teachers either to study such a concept or to quit teaching.
Agatha, at first, is overcome with mirth at the absurdity of Parilee's
situation; but she soon realizes that it is not absurd at all. On the contrary, "it was logical, even predictable; it was exactly the sort of im-
passe a group of ignorant lawmakers would stumble into; and it was
precisely characteristic of Miss Parilee that she should pick out the
harsh medieval clause in the statute and consider that an advanced
educational idea" (42).

As Stribling did in *Teeftallow*, he brings out in *Bright Metal* the
fear and the superstition of hill-country Calvinism as it grinds down
on the people who hold to its tenets. Agatha's educated mind, of
course, rebels against such a debilitating religion. She is horrified to
hear a hill man, who has killed a neighbor over a two-dollar mistake
in an account book caused by a fly speck that made a three appear to
be a five, lay the whole unfortunate episode at God's feet with the
assertion that, "God meant for Sam to die and fer me to spend the
rest o' my days in misery, Miss Pomeroy. We didn't live right neither
one of us. And to show His power, He done it with a little fly speck"
(165). Shocked by such an inhuman philosophy, Agatha is
nevertheless unable to offer the comfort of her modern skepticism as

an antidote to the fixed religious ideas of the old man. When he points out to her that, even if he is hanged for murder, he knows that he will be saved because he has felt God in his heart, she recognizes a kind of defensive psychology even in such a terrible and inhuman faith; for all who believed in it held themselves among the elect.

Another facet of hill life that Stribling focuses on in *Bright Metal*, one that he later developed more fully in the trilogy, is the southern code — that romantic and chivalric set of attitudes and practices prevalent in the South. For Agatha, such a code does not seem so romantic and chivalric; she regards it as a delimiting force that rejects individual judgment and mechanizes human relations. She sees an example of this code when Pom gets involved in a brawl over a hog and a dog and then shoots the dog (his own) because in the melee the dog accidentally bit Agatha's hand. Even dogs are not allowed to err and injure one of the family.

In Stribling's treatment of the southern code, he sees it as growing out of the religious viewpoint in the South. Holding religion as a matter of pure faith results in holding it as a code of irrationalism. Transposed to the social scheme, it becomes a code that replaces responsibility with authority. This situation is what Agatha comes to understand — and to reject.

Agatha meets two persons who do not conform to the standard hill pattern; and the first, Risdale Balus, is a young hill man, who, with the possible exception of Agatha, is the best-developed character in the novel. Unlike most of the other hill people in Lane County, Risdale is a questioner, wondering on all manner of things — whether the brand put on a colt grows as the colt grows or merely stays the same size. While Mrs. Pomeroy thinks such a question is foolish, Agatha appreciates Risdale's inquiring mind. Contrasted with Parilee's "quaking study of biology," Risdale's question represents a kind of twentieth-century reformation. Combining the usual stoicism of the hill man with a sensitivity that, at least in Stribling's novels, is scarce in the hills, Risdale seems to have come to terms with life. He lives in the present and has no sense of the past and only a vague yearning for the future — "a whole-souled Pan who would live everywhere as fully as the accidents of life allowed" (234 - 35).

The other person Agatha meets who stands outside the accepted pattern of hill society is Colonel Brierly-Thornton, a senile remnant of the old southern aristocracy. He has no use for Yankees nor for the hill people, whom he condescendingly refers to as the "poor whites."

In their hands, the southern code has, he feels, become degraded. When Fatty Bobbs threatens to kill Risdale on sight, the colonel sees such a situation as a corruption of code *duellum* that flourished in the days of chivalry and in the early history of the South. The hill man, instead of sending a note by a second and of appointing a place of meeting, for example, is content to kill his opponent by surprise anywhere and any way he can.

With Agatha, Risdale, the colonel, and the hill people in general, Stribling presents four views of life: the liberated view of Agatha, the questioning yet basically hill-country oriented view of Risdale, the southern aristocratic view of the colonel, and the socially narrow and religiously fatalistic view of the hill people. Stated another way, these views represent past tradition (the colonel), the present limited by the past (the hill people), a vague yearning for the future (Risdale), and the future (Agatha). Seen chronologically, these views represent to Stribling the evolutionary process of life and society. If any change is to come to the hill country, it will come through people like Risdale and Agatha — especially the latter, since she has a clearer vision of a different kind of life.

The women of Lane County stand in stark contrast to Agatha's vision. She cannot understand why these women take no interest in the local political scene and the corruptive influences pervading it. Moreover, she is depressed at the superficial and mechanical attempts the women make at conversation. Their talk centers on most occasions on the rearing of children; and, when it does, Agatha realizes as she never has before "her own implicit femaleness. It brought her to the lowliness of a reproducing machine, a contrivance life used as it passed along" (97). Even when Constable Boggs shoots a Negro just outside the window of the house where the Ladies Christian Workers Society is meeting, the discussion it elicits from the members, though lively and vociferous, is merely a nervous reaction to restore their equilibrium, upset by the shock of the shooting. Agatha feels pity and anger at the "epochs of social suppression that lay back of these women whose outraged sense of justice produced simple chatter to settle their own nerves instead of a remedial action" (105). She recognizes that an individual can be constructive or destructive only in so far as society permits him to be; and in the South, women, by virtue of the customs established for their protection, have little maneuverability outside the home. The word "lady" is thrust at Agatha so persistently and so automatically that she feels "as if someone were winding silk about her and admiring its hue and texture in warm terms, but at the same time was binding her hand and foot" (114).

Agatha has some success in arousing the women of the society; but, as they leave the Pomeroy house after laying plans to use their votes against Bobbs in the coming election, Agatha is struck by the image of the small group as it is juxtaposed against the magnitude and splendor of the sky and the fields: "Their shapeless figures were subordinated to the bravura of the sky and the solemn dark chords of the fields. They looked so small, moving carefully among the puddles lest they muddy their feet; and the sunset flaunted so vast and indifferent to them — a handful of shabby women scattering over the countryside with notions of some great vague reform in their unpracticed heads" (109). Just how far apart Agatha is from these hill women is apparent when Parilee, looking at the same scene, remarks, "I don't know how this'll turn out, Agatha, but if God is with us, who can be against us" (109)? The sunset may comfort Parilee, but it arouses in Agatha the feeling of being "dwarfed by its infinite indifference to her hopes, her morality, and her existence" (109).

Agatha is never quite clear in her mind as to why she wants to get involved in politics. As we have already noted, she is not a lofty idealist like Carol Kennicutt, though there is idealism in her, as Colonel Brierly-Thornton sees. But hers is an idealism that will not of its own accord burst into flame; it needs an outside force for its ignition — and the hill country becomes this force. New York, to Agatha, seems "simple and idyllic compared to the strictness and forearmings and personal compromises and moral squirmings of Lane County folk" (223). Although corruption in politics is hardly less prevalent in New York than in Lane County (as Stribling shows in *The Sound Wagon*), the anonymity and the freedom of that city would allow a person like Agatha a chance to develop with few restrictions. In Lane County, however, she is trapped in a society in which primary relationships are important and often overriding. Rather than attempting to understand the social and political situations into which she has been thrust, she becomes critical of them.

But to say that Agatha is critical of Lane County and its ways merely because she does not understand them is too simple an explanation. Agatha — a young woman vibrant with the force of life, in much the same way as Cissie is in *Birthright* — serves as a counter to the force of materialism that has taken over in Lane County (and in the whole South). Only on occasion is she consciously aware of this clash of forces and then of only one side of it. She sees Pom's cotton gin as a symbol of his materialistic interests and as a cause of his neglect and misunderstanding of her. She also sees politics subverted by the individual politicians who hope for material gain. Buckingham Sharp, the lawyer, offers her perhaps the best illustration of the trend toward materialism when he recalls to her that the psychology he studied in school was divided into the Will, the Soul, and the Emotions — a mystical kind of psychology but one that, in his youth, meant something. Yet, when Agatha asks why he came to Lane County, his response is not at all mystical: "To make some ready money, Mrs. Pomeroy, so I could establish myself in a city. I think the most insidious thing in the world is a small success" (147). Colonel Brierly-Thornton also has an insight into what is happening, but his explanations are couched in the clichés with which the remnants of southern aristocracy look back on the halcyon days; and they thus have little relevancy for Agatha.

The other side of this clash between the forces of life and materialism is never logically understood by Agatha. Something instinctive with her, something that wells up from her whole being, it is at its strongest when she is with Risdale; for his elemental vitality is in close harmony with her own. And on this basis she gives herself to him in a scene of lovemaking that, juxtaposed against the code of the hill country, is natural and refreshing. When it is over, there is no pretense and no regret. Such a relationship, however, cannot be permanent; and both Agatha and Risdale know it.

Agatha is no match for the astute politicians whom she is attempting to unseat; and, in the end, she must reconcile herself to the fact that whatever change comes to the social or political life of the hill country must come slowly and not in one great leap. Her first reaction is to take her (and Pom's) child and return to the North, where she feels that little Pom will have a better opportunity than he would ever have in Lane County to grow up with a wider vision of life. On the bus into Lanesburg, she meets a woman from the North who is coming to teach in Lane County and who maintains that she will teach evolution because she feels somebody must tell the hill people the truth. To Agatha's question about what the truth is, she responds, "Evolution is the orderly development of life from inchoate beginnings" (450). These comments from a stranger — comments that stem from the same kind of view that Agatha has held about the hill country — develop in the girl's mind thoughts that, prior to her recent experiences in Lane County, she could never have had. She sees that the only truth is a pragmatic truth, a theory that will enable a person to go on with life.

In one sense, Agatha's defeat is a victory. Like Peter Siner, she has come full circle. There is no single explanation or remedy for the social ills of the South. With this understanding, Agatha calls Pom to come to Lanesburg and take her back. The ending of the novel has all the ingredients of a rebirth image — "the new moon, like the end of a little silver cradle, lodged in the dark lacework of the courthouse trees" (453), the rain falling, and the baby asleep at the girl's bosom. But it is more an image of continuation than of rebirth: there is no return to innocence, nor is there any arrival at definitive knowledge through experience; it is not a beginning nor an ending, but a going on. Just as the moon waxes and wanes and just as the earth with its mysterious tides spins on into time and space, humanity too moves in its own ways — toward what, no one knows.

## II    *An Arkansas Tale*

Stribling did not consider *Backwater* one of his serious novels, either before or after it was completed. The historical trilogy was taking form in his mind while he was writing this novel, and he intended it more as a "pot boiler" than anything else. Having extensively treated the hill country of Tennessee in three previous novels, there was not much more he was interested in doing with that area, so he shifted the setting for *Backwater* to Arkansas — to a town called Ringerman, located on the Mississippi River. The novel has little to recommend it, beyond one or two good scenes and two fairly well drawn characters. There are no penetrating social views, such as one finds in *Birthright, Teeftallow,* or *Bright Metal,* and little if any satire.

The main character in the novel is Jim Murdock, son of Bill Jack Murdock, plantation owner and bootlegger — but predominantly a "moonshiner." Jim, who has just graduated from agricultural college, is trying to free himself from the connotations of the family name. He is in love with Mary Sue Meredith and she with him, but she cannot accept him as a husband because he does not come from a good family. Eventually, however, she raises herself above the trivialities of family name and manners to rescue Jim and his father from a group of irate citizens who are beating the two men because of Bill Jack's bootlegging. Exhilarated by the excitement of the moment, Mary Sue realizes that she is now not afraid of what might

happen to her name through her association with the Murdocks —
and we have the conventional happy ending.

Neither Jim nor Mary Sue is well drawn as a character, but Bill
Jack Murdock and Pontius Pilt, a Negro hand on the Murdock plantation, are. Especially colorful is Bill Jack, a hard-shell Baptist who
believes that the law is like a fence: "You can step over it to take a
short cut somewheres, then when you git there you can step back in
again."[2] A true descendant of the frontier, Bill Jack justifies his
bootlegging both religiously and economically. If he does not make
liquor, the men will go outside the county to get it, thus taking
money away from where it is needed to run business. Moreover, his
liquor has never made anybody paralyzed nor blind; and he feels
that he is protecting hundreds of drinkers "jest by stayin' in the
whiskey business. And 'y gannies, Jim, as a Baptist and a Democrat I
ain't a-goin' to shirk my duty for my ease" (43).

The best part of the novel comes near the end as the town of
Ringerman fights to keep the flooding Mississippi River from breaking the levee. In a sternly naturalist vein, Stribling pictures men as
swarming over the imperiled levee like ants in a disturbed anthill:
"Teams of tiny mules swung up on the shoe string and dumped
scoops of dirt and stone and then swung down again out of sight into
the bowl of Ringerman. Endless little black men worked with tiny
picks and shovels. Only from a great distance did Jim Murdock
realize how tiny and unimportant was Ringerman in comparison
with the shoreless sea that washed its dyke" (253). In this elemental
struggle between man and nature, the river symbolizes the un-
leashed power of an indifferent universe as it pours through the
broken dyke.

While neither *Bright Metal* nor *Backwater* reaches the artistic
level of *Teeftallow*, the former does clearly present the counter-
education of an individual who believes in a set of ideals that has little relevance in the small southern town in which she finds herself.
Agatha Pomeroy, like Carol Kennicutt in Sinclair Lewis's *Main
Street*, suffers disillusionment; but, unlike Carol, Agatha recovers
from her disillusionment. Stribling does not leave the reader with
the impression that Agatha's life will be marked by bitterness as a
result of her experiences. On the contrary, the final impression is
that she will go on to make a meaningful life for herself and her
family. *Bright Metal*, then, is one of Stribling's more optimistic
works.

## CHAPTER 6

# Ordeal by Fire

STRIBLING'S trilogy — *The Forge*, and *The Unfinished Cathe-dral* — represents his best efforts at novel writing and has as its basic theme the social change in the South resulting from the Civil War and the end of slavery. *The Forge* (1931) covers the war and the period of Reconstruction; *The Store* (1932), the years following Reconstruction; and *The Unfinished Cathedral* (1933), the early 1920s. The unifying thread that runs through all three books is the history of the Vaiden family for three generations; beginning with old Jimmie Vaiden, a plantation owner, it ends with Marsan Vaiden, old Jimmie's granddaughter through his son Miltiades. Actually, Miltiades dominates *The Store* and much of *The Unfinished Cathedral* as he lives through the new social and economic changes occurring in the South. In addition to the Vaidens, Stribling pictures Negroes (slave and free), including quadroons and octoroons; large plantation owners; poor-white sharecroppers; small farmers; ministers; religious mystics; Yankee soldiers; carpetbaggers; members of the Ku Klux Klan; politicians; grasping storekeepers; and pushing real-estate men.

Stribling called *The Forge* "the story of the dissolution of a Southern family which vanished during the [Civil] war" — a story that "cuts through the strata of the South, the aristocracy, the middle class, the poor whites and the Negroes. It's an unhappy sort of novel, an effort to show the interaction of these various classes."[1] Covering the period from the eve of the Civil War through the early days of Reconstruction, *The Forge* is a "big" novel, the most ambitious that Stribling had tried to that time. Few facets of southern life of the time are not touched upon in the 525 pages that cover the dissolution of a social order and the beginning of a new one. Told episodically through events concerning various members of the Vaiden family, as they are caught in the social upheaval of the Civil

War, the novel has no single plot line. As a result, there is no one
protagonist in the precise sense of the term — though Stribling does
introduce Miltiades Vaiden, who is more or less the main character
in the second and third books of the trilogy.

## I  *Antebellum Days*

The opening of *The Forge* presents a picture of the Vaiden family
and their plantation. Old man Jimmie Vaiden was a pioneer — a
blacksmith before he became a landed man — and the forge that
stands across the rutted road from his house attests to his rise from a
tradesman to a small planter. The house itself, "half a house and half
a fort," is an example of the frontier flavor of northern Alabama on
the eve of the Civil War. Jimmie had built his house with "the un-
planning certitude of a wasp,"[2] and the house reflects the life that
revolves around it, a life based on the casualness and chance of
nature.

Close to nature as they are, the Vaidens are not living in a pastoral
paradise in complete harmony with their environment or with one
another. On the contrary, the uncertain human relationships and the
lack of personal discipline apparent in the life on the Vaiden plantation stands in distinct contrast to the gentility and order on the
larger, more aristocratic neighboring plantations. Individually, the
lives of the members of the family are complicated by a typical frontier relationship of independence from one another, each member
acting selfishly and often at cross purposes with another. Products of
their environment and of their religious beliefs, they believe in
states' rights and in individual determination of all legal and moral
questions. And neither they nor their God ever forgives anybody
anything.

As a hard-shell Baptist, Jimmie Vaiden believes in water for his
soul and whiskey for his body; and, throughout the novel, he has
nothing but harsh words for the members of his family. Not an
aristocrat, he nevertheless identifies himself with that class. The
Union to him is a voluntary political structure, and any state that so
desires should be allowed to withdraw. He justifies slavery by refer-
ring to the Bible and is in his glory when he vehemently discusses
this question with Parson Mulry, both men having the fondness for
the rhetoric typical of southerners. Their biblical arguments justify-
ing slavery explain the entire pattern of life around them and un-
derline their belief that Negroes were indeed predestined to be
slaves.

The Vaidens are quick to assert their superiority over their slaves, but there is little in their actions to confirm their right to do so on any basis other than that of ownership. Entrusted, in theory at least, with the safety of the Negroes on their plantation, they contribute — at times purposely and always without hesitation — to the precariousness of the Negroes' existence. Orders given by one Vaiden are often countermanded by another. For example, Augustus and Polycarp, the two teenage brothers in the family, take from the ploughs the two mules that they want to ride to a dance and explain over the expostulations of the field hands that their father need not be burdened with the granting of permission. "Trouble is," one hand complains, "when you take a small bu'den off'n his shouldahs, he puts a la'ge bull whop onto ouahs" (45) — nor is the punishment meted out to the slaves consistent. Old Jimmie vents his wrath on a Negro for a trifling matter and then lets something serious go unpunished. He is most infuriated whenever one of his slaves attempts to slip away when he is called, for the old man sees the whole social system of the South as depending upon not letting the Negroes escape.

The Negroes on the Vaiden plantation are depicted as typically ignorant and superstitious, except for their acknowledged leader, the ancient Aunt Creasy, whose enviable placidity has evolved from years of toil and tribulation and whose eternal wisdom is as soothing as the liniment that she rubs into beaten Negroes' wounds. When the slave George steals a silver spoon from the big house and makes it into a bullet to kill white people, he is caught trying to slip away from old Jimmie. Though he is whipped, his silver bullet goes undiscovered. As Aunt Creasy treats his lashed back, we are made aware of superstition, attitudes of defiance, resignation to social status, and the acceptance of color as the key element of southern life. George proudly boasts of the power his silver bullet gives him over white people, but the philosophic Aunt Creasy sagely points out to him that a white person's own spoon will not allow itself to become an instrument with which a slave can then kill that very white person.

This particular scene depresses the quadroon Gracie, one of the best-drawn characters in the novel. Old Jimmie Vaiden's daughter through miscegenation, she regards George with a "feeling of the racial blank back of him — and of herself. They were both like rabbits that sprang from under their feet in the cotton rows, without father or mother, without sons or daughters" (37). George's whipping brings into sharp focus for her the Negro's position in the South, a position that makes her and her slave husband Solomon nothing more than animals, destined only to work and to breed.

These thoughts become a reality when Miltiades Vaiden, as his father did to the quadroon's mother, rapes Gracie in the barn, saying, "What difference does it make to you, what sort of husband —" (161). Gracie, wishing she could fling away her whole generative organ, looks to Aunt Creasy for understanding and comfort; but the old woman, recalling an experience that she had had on a slave ship in her youth, can only philosophically echo what Miltiades had said as he ravished the girl: "What dif'funce do hit make who you' young un's pappy is? Woman has to have he'p to have chillun. Man lak all othah men . . . niggah woman has to take who comes an' go on" (165). The seed that Miltiades plants in Gracie, however, causes him anguish later in *The Store* and in *The Unfinished Cathedral*.

In the Vaiden household, the eldest daughter, Cassandra, whose authority is more certain than that of her Greek namesake, acts as the real head of the family. She best understands old Jimmie's unorthodox behavior and how to cope with it. She is able, for example, to advise her sister Marcia just the right moment to ask for the horse Joe to ride to a neighboring plantation. None of the Vaiden offspring, for that matter, with the exception of Miltiades, does anything without first getting permission from Cassandra: Marcia asks to wear a new dress to a party; Marcia asks to marry A. Gray Lacefield; Polycarp and Augustus do not enlist in the Confederate army at their first opportunity, because they have not asked Cassandra.

Despite the power she wields over the family, Cassandra is essentially a negative person. After telling Polycarp, for example, that Ponny BeShears is not good enough for a Vaiden to marry, she describes a perfect wife for her brother — one so completely composed of negatives that "Polycarp was not only to be most lonely when most surrounded by his family," but also, "when he married this perfect creature of Miss Cassandra's continued subtractions, he would be, to all intents and purposes, alone" (117). Cassandra seems destined to play a leading role, but she never does. She is unable to separate herself from her environment and her bluestocking family pride. As a result, her urging of Marcia to "improve her mind" and her own reading of Thomas Paine's *The Rights of Man* become nothing but sheer irony. She does have the strength of purpose to teach Gracie to read (against Southern law at that time) — not, however, from any feeling for Gracie, but rather for practical reasons and for proof of her own strong will. Cassandra, in another place or another time, might well have been a crusading woman; but, in antebellum Alabama, she is confined by her father's stern, unforgiving God and by the social conditions of the South. By viewing the whole southern complex as part of God's will, she, like many other Stribling characters, can absolve herself from all responsibility and become merely a passive observer.

Marcia, Cassandra's younger sister, presents a striking contrast. Though Stribling never definitely gives her age, she is probably around sixteen. Of all the Vaiden family, she is the only person, with the possible exceptions of Laura (old Jimmie's wife) and Polycarp, who evidences any capacity for true feeling. In her, we see the first glimpse of a strain of Vaiden blood that will, in *The Unfinished Cathedral*, come to fuller fruition with Marsan Vaiden, Miltiades' daughter. Marcia, the sentimental romantic, is a beautiful girl whose dominant vision of herself is as the martyred heroine who surrenders all for her lover. A secondary vision has her making entrances and exits in a flowing dress on the graceful staircase of a plantation manor. Yet there is a quality in Marcia that prevents us from dismissing her as a mere romantic girl and nothing more. She does, like the rest of her family, accept the social system of the South and does enjoy the leisure that it offers; but she feels that slaveholders have an obligation to their slaves — actually, a kind of spiritual relationship in which Negroes are considered as a part of the owner's family.

Perhaps the one act that redeems Marcia from being marked as just a romantic dreamer is her decision near the end of the book to go away with Jerry Catlin, the Tennessee hill man who serves in the Union army and is captured by the Confederates. Giving up her coming marriage to the aristocrat A. Gray Lacefield, she asks Cassandra to tell him that she loves him but that Jerry needs her. There is, of course, a touch of romantic sentimentality here, but the importance of the incident lies in its reflection of Stribling's idea that the progress of any race depends upon the woman's having complete freedom in choosing her mate — the theory that Peter Siner formulates in *Birthright*. Certainly, we see Jerry Catlin as a much more substantial person than A. Gray Lacefield, and we can only think that Marcia sees this also — making her choice on that basis. Lacefield would only complement the romantic side of Marcia, but Jerry will bring out that side of her that makes more of the southern tradition than a mere figment of materialism. The offspring of their union is the Jerry Catlin of *The Store* and *The Unfinished Cathedral*, a deeply thinking, perceptive person.

Stribling, then, presents in Marcia, though somewhat sporadically, some of the finest characteristics of southern womanhood. She is temperamental and a bit spoiled; but, when she can escape the iron hand of Calvinism which holds the Vaiden plantation in its relentless grip, she emerges to significant dimensions. Particularly does she do so when she visits the Lacefield plantation — a place that makes her existence at home and the existence of such families as the BeShears, the Hams, and the Dalrymples seem "but a prologue to this warm full-bodied reality" (77).

During her visits to the Lacefields, she is sensitive and mature, a desirable young woman courted by the son of the household and complimented by the glamorous and discerning Colonel Emory Crowninshield. It is as if the genteel and chivalric air of the Lacefield plantation nourishes Marcia at the same time that it stultifies southern society in general. Marcia believes that a girl's worth inheres strictly in her own personal qualities, but she does not fully comprehend these qualities. She feels them in herself, "vague excellencies — a power of romance, idealization, industry in the service of her beloved, loyalty, a selfless tenderness" (78).

The world of the Lacefield manor offers a distinct contrast to that of the Vaiden "half-house half-fort," for it is the ideal South of John Esten Cooke and Thomas Nelson Page. As Marcia and her two brothers ride out of the hills into the Reserve, they get a composite picture of this different world, complete with lush fields, manor houses flanked by slave quarters, and chanting slaves. In such a world even a member of the Vaiden family, although merely the hired overseer, assumes the dashing appearance of a cavalier. From a distance, Miltiades Vaiden is a "trim, broad-shouldered figure on a shining black horse" (66), whose thoroughbred mount gracefully jumps a fence in practice for a forthcoming fox hunt. In conversation, he exhibits un-Vaiden-like traits of tact with his brother and generosity with his sister, along with admirable self-control and an exceptional talent with Negroes — traits that strike Marcia as fine and aristocratic. Here again Stribling shows that environment makes the man; and there is no better example of this idea than Miltiades Vaiden, who becomes the venerable Colonel Milt of the next two volumes of the trilogy.

At the Lacefields, we are introduced to Emory Crowninshield, intellectual and would-be politician, whom Stribling uses as a spokesman for the aristocratic South and whose explanation of slavery offers a graphic example of another facet of the southern rationalization of that institution. To Marcia's complaint about Alex-BeShears's selling Gracie's husband away from his bride, Crown-inshield explains such a deed in terms of compensation, rationalizing that such is the price the South must pay for the beautiful and gracious life that it seeks to support.

The South, in Crowninshield's eyes (and the eyes of all southerners like him), is to become through the labor of the Negro and through secession from the Union "a nation like Mercury, new-lighted on a heaven-kissing hill" (81). In contrast with the North, conditioned by materialism, the South is creating a way of life. Merely a desire to "mold something out of life itself," however, would appear the most fragile of threads that a nation could weave into the uncertain fabric of its economic existence; and Marcia asks whether the South will ever have to pay for its "original sin" of slavery. Crowninshield responds that slavery has both its good and its bad side and that they can only hope that these two sides will balance out in the end. The irony of such a response is apparent when, a moment later, a messenger rides in with the news that Fort Sumter has fallen; for the South is already on the road to retribution.

## II  *Origins of a New South*

With the news of Fort Sumter, the lives of all the Vaidens and Lacefields are engulfed in feverish war hysteria. In this first phase of the dissolution of the Old South, Stribling makes us aware that not all southerners went to war for the same reasons. A striking difference exists, for instance, between old Jimmie Vaiden's shooting his anvil not only in celebration of the fall of Sumter but also in a tribute to his hell-fire and brimstone God that foreordained slavery and Caruther Lacefield's comment to Marcia that she is the reason why the gallant men of the South are going to war. To them, she is the saint on the altar. The image of the Confederate soldier drawn by Stribling, however, is not Cooke's dashing young cavalier, complete with French sabre and black plume; Stribling's Confederate army is a conglomeration of recruits in various garb and armed with whatever weapons they happen to own, "training for glory in the midst of their jolly youth" (103).

Stribling grew up on stories of the war told by his Union father and his Confederate uncles. He himself, moreover, spent a month at Shiloh — where his father was wounded and captured — walking over the battlefield and through the cemeteries to relive the battle in his mind so that he could use it in *The Forge*. This background, coupled with his descriptive abilities, enabled Stribling to present a battle scene in the novel that, in many respects, resembles such scenes in Stephen Crane's *The Red Badge of Courage*.

In *The Forge*, Stribling also brings out the attitudes of that segment of southern society that remained loyal to the Union; and, in doing so, he again drew on his own background to present a picture of the Catlin family, Tennessee hill people who are not slaveholders and are not in sympathy with the Confederacy. Only forty miles separates the Catlins from the Vaidens and the Lacefields, but the gulf between their social views is wide indeed. Augustus Vaiden, on his way to join the Confederate army, falls into the hands of a group of marauders who are about to steal the Catlin horses and cattle. Augustus escapes and warns the Catlins, and they in return provide him food and lodging. Mr. Catlin scolds Augustus for wanting to fight to preserve slavery, an institution forbidden by the word of God. Mrs. Catlin, however, accepts the irony of geographic location and points out to her husband that "if you lived forty miles furder South, reason an' the word of God would tell you to chain up niggers an' work the daylights out of 'em" (193). Her thoughts are similar to those of Emory Crowninshield when he explains to Marcia Vaiden that "if we were born North we would act exactly as the Northern people do" (82).

The war brings into focus a conglomeration of varied interests and purposes in the South which otherwise would never have been exposed or recognized. Augustus, for example, had always supposed that politics, like religion, was something handed down from on high; and he is dumbfounded when he hears his friend Gillie Dilliehay explain that it was only his father's accidental possession of a slave received as payment of a debt that made him, Gillie, a Confederate. To Augustus's comment that one should hardly change his politics over so small a thing as a debt, Gillie reasons that the threat of losing property is sufficient reason, since laws exist to protect property.

When Gillie is next seen, his loyalties have become even more questionable, since he is now with the Union army. Jerry Catlin tries to justify this switch of sides to Marcia, explaining that Gillie found the Yankees received better food and pay than did the Confederates and that his extra pay over two years would more than pay for the loss of his father's slave. Marcia is shocked and incensed that a man could have no more principles than to be concerned only with eating and making money. But, as is true with so many of Stribling's characters, Marcia is unaware that she has based her own views upon an illusion. She sees Miltiades, for example, as a symbol of all that is fine in southern manhood; but, after the war, he becomes the leader of the Ku Klux Klan in its most nefarious activities. Moreover, of the several marriages in the novel, his to Ponny BeShears is the only one made for money.

Materialism, however, touches not only the South. When the Vaiden slaves are to be sold to pay the household debts, Gracie escapes to the Union army and rides south with them, watching along the way her former neighbors' houses burning (both plantation houses and Negro cabins). Inquiring of a Yankee lieutenant as to why the "Army of the Lord," with the ostensible purpose of helping Negro slaves, should burn houses the slaves lived in, Gracie is told that economics, not compassion for slaves, is the real reason for the war. Gracie also learns that, though she is free, she is still being used when the lieutenant tells her that he has a pretty dress for her and that he will bring it around to her that night. The only real difference is that she now gets silk hose and pretty dresses in exchange for the favors of her body.

The slaves in general are caught between conflicting loyalties: loyalty to their masters and loyalty to their own freedom. When the Vaiden cotton gin is set afire by Yankee soldiers, for example, Stribling's description of the scene produces a mixed feeling of comedy and pathos as both Vaidens and slaves attempt to put out the fire, with the aged Aunt Creasy squatting over the last sparks and urinating them out. Another instance of slave loyalty occurs when Gillie Dilliehay's slave Abraham plans to follow his master into battle to "he'p Mas' Dilliehay keep me" (200). His idea is to be near so that he can go to Gillie's aid if the latter gets hit.

Even when the war is over, the Negroes seem not to comprehend fully what is happening to the social order under which they have been living; as a result, they become easy victims for exploiting carpetbaggers. When the ex-Vaiden slave George is told he is to run for political office and could come to be called the Honorable George Vaiden, he responds, "Oh, my Gawd . . . de Honahble Gawge Vaiden" (405), and breaks down in laughter.

At the end of *The Forge*, Stribling leaves us with the knowledge that an era has ended for the Vaidens, the Lacefields, and the whole South. Marcia Vaiden, in her moment of truth, realizes that the gallant soldiers of the South have been responsible for the emaciated condition of Jerry Catlin. She sweeps away the former lines of demarcation and decides to mingle rebel blood with Union blood. A. Gray Lacefield is to become a newspaper man; his aristocratic father gives up his plantation in favor of a smaller house in Florence; and Augustus and Rose Vaiden decide to open a boarding house in the town. Miltiades Vaiden, who had once planned to marry Drusilla Lacefield and carry on the Lacefield plantation, is now financially destitute. He realizes that he must seek another way to achieve success, and he knows too that the Negro will be a key element in any plan that he formulates — that the man who bought from them and sold to them would in all probability be the man who would finally receive their earnings. Such a man, thinks Miltiades, would be quite different from the plantation slaveholder; he would need to be unscrupulous and clever. Miltiades recognizes the irony in the situation: the power held so long and so genteelly by the plantation owners would be taken over by tradesmen and shopkeepers, by men like Handback and Alex BeShears, whose only interest would be the making of money. As if to make the break with his past ideals complete, Miltiades marries Ponny BeShears, Alex's daughter, hoping that he will be able eventually to inherit whatever the grasping merchant has accumulated.

The final scene of the novel is powerful in its dramatic irony and in its pathos. Old Jimmie Vaiden, impoverished and bereft of his senses, attempts to light a fire for his forge; and, in doing so, he suffers a stroke. Gracie, the quadroon, comes to him as he lies calling for his daughter Marcia. When Gracie tells him that Marcia is gone, Jimmie mumbles that he wants to die in the arms of his daughter. Gracie explains that he is indeed dying in the arms of his daughter, though not Marcia. Jimmie cannot accept this fact, and calling Gracie a "nigger," he pushes her face away and dies.

### III   The Forge — *More than a Social Document*

The first American novel to be selected by the English Book League, *The Forge* represents Stribling's best literary effort up to that time. Marked by humor, irony, and objectivity, *The Forge*, as social documentation, hits hard and cuts clean; and in doing so it represents a significant step forward in the treatment of the tragic complexities of the South both during and immediately following the Civil War. Relying on his intended and appropriate strategy of episodic structure and generally stock characterization, Stribling created a novel that unflinchingly lays out for the reader the social, political, and economic fabric of a section that was undergoing changes that were at once subtle and traumatic.

Even though the book was a best-seller and was praised by Theodore Dreiser as an excellent example of American realistic writing, there were some reviewers who saw it in a lesser light. In a kind of humorous response to such reviewers, Stribling wrote the following:

The different things critics condemn in my novels are always interesting to me, and once in awhile informative. I mean things I may be able to remedy the next time. Sometimes they are not. For instance, when Herschel Brickell complains sadly that I have no style, well, that's the end of that. I just haven't and Brickell and I will have to let that pass; or at least I will.

Also I am finding out a number of very reputable and famous (although dead) writers, who I am not. One of my critics complains that I am no Tolstoy and that I have not given the world another *War and Peace*. He says, "What is wanted, of course, is some philosophy of history, some imaginative conception large enough to embrace the causes of the North and the South in the Civil War, some suggestion of the apocalyptic tricks of history." Now if I had had those things I would have been like Tolstoy; but if Tolstoy hadn't had 'em he would have sold like me.

Another fellow dealt very drastically with me because I was no Anatole France. He said I was enigmatic. In fact his charge against me was enigmatism. He said I was funny when he did not understand why I should be funny and serious when he did not understand why I should be serious. (This is the first known instance of a critic admitting there was something he did not know, but of course that was only inductively and by indirection.) He went on in the same strain and could not fathom why I should be humorous with a character on one page and serious with him on the next, although, undoubtedly, this critic treats, in exactly this fashion every day in the year, his friends, his wife, his children, and himself — possibly not himself. And at this point comes in his charge that I am not Anatole France. He says France was constantly bitter. France treated the human race as a breed of beetles all the time. Now would it clear my skirts if I admitted my guilt and agreed that I did not always consider the human race as beetles? They become men and women ever and anon, with, of course, the exceptions of one or two who remain consistently beetleish.

Still another critic said a lot of nice things about *The Forge*. He said it was full of action, humor, pathos, surprises, etc., but he says: "It is just a novel after all." Well now, there you are! What are you going to say to that? I started out to write a novel, now this fellow charges that I have written one. I am as hopeless as a bootlegger with the goods on him.[3]

CHAPTER 7

# The Ashes of Tradition

ON August 6, 1930, less than one month after he completed *The Forge*, Stribling married Lou Ella Kloss, a girl he had known since his childhood in Clifton. After a wedding trip to New York, Tom and Lou Ella went to Florida for the winter. They spent the next three years between New York in the summers and Fort Myers, Florida, in the winters. In Fort Myers, the couple rented a house in a deserted orange grove, complete with snakes, birds, and all the grapefruit and oranges they could eat. The house was so remote that, in the beginning, the rental agent was often called to get the Striblings to their house after they had gotten lost. This was the first time Stribling ever had a really quiet place to write, and he wrote there the second novel of the trilogy, *The Store*.

Basically, *The Store* is the story of Miltiades Vaiden's rise from poverty to riches during the years following Reconstruction. Forty-eight years old at the beginning of the novel, he is morose and discontent, living idly on an insufficient income with his wife Ponny, the girl he had married at the end of *The Forge* for what little money she had inherited. He is waiting for an opportunity to take the social and financial position which he feels he deserves. His chance comes when he discovers that J. Handback, a store owner whose earlier bankruptcy had brought about Miltiades' financial ruin, has been sleeping with the quadroon Gracie. Blackmailing Handback into giving him a job, he soon becomes overseer of his plantations. Feeling that Handback still owes him something, Miltiades steals five hundred bales of the store owner's cotton, sells it in New Orleans, and hides the money from the sale with the one person he knows he can trust, Gracie.

When Handback and the sheriff go to Miltiades' house with a search warrant while he is away, they frighten his pregnant wife into a miscarriage that causes her death. As a result, Handback is willing to drop criminal charges against Miltiades in return for a payment of ten thousand dollars from the forty-eight thousand dollars received for the stolen cotton. Thus, ironically enough, his wife's death not only frees him from a marriage he was not happy with but also keeps him from jail and provides him with a small fortune. He establishes himself in the mercantile business and eventually marries Sydna Crowninshield, daughter of Drusilla Lacefield Crowninshield, to whom he had been engaged before the war (in *The Forge*). Tragedy strikes near the end of the novel when Toussaint Vaiden, Gracie's son by Miltiades, is lynched for a rape he did not commit. Miltiades does not learn that the man is his own son until it is too late to prevent the lynching. Within this narrative framework, then, Stribling brings in various other characters and incidents that compose the social complex of Florence, Alabama, in the 1880s.

## I  *The New South*

When Jerry Catlin II, son of Jerry and Marcia (Vaiden) Catlin, arrives in Florence, Alabama, he remembers the innumerable tales told him by his mother of that ancient and magnificent world which she had known as a girl. The world that Marcia knew, however, is gone. All that remains of it are museumlike hallways with their ancient furniture and brass lion's-foot door bells that do not ring but merely rattle feebly. The time is 1885, and the South, impoverished by the Civil War and its ill-managed aftermath, is in the process of charting a new course socially, economically, and spiritually for itself. Gone are the large plantations with their auspicious manor houses and their aristocratic social patterns. Gone also are the smaller planters (like the Vaidens of *The Forge*). The town has now become the center of southern economic and social life — and it is a far cry from the leisurely paradise of the Old South, where time "eddied round and round and did not follow anywhere."[1]

The fact of the Old South may be gone, but the ideal of it is not. Pine Street in Florence still maintains an air of the old order with its stately oaks, chirping birds, and fragrant magnolias. Some of the residents of the street — Drusilla Crowninshield, for example — are able to maintain the pretense of gracious living. Drusilla, who cannot really afford servants, is able to staff her home with unpaid domestics by training young Negro girls in the fine points of serving.

The white view of Negroes, moreover, has not changed. Indeed, if anything, the end of slavery has stiffened the white attitude and made life even more difficult for the Negroes than it was in antebellum days. No longer chattel slaves, they are still at the economic mercy of the whites. People like J. Handback may have been forced into bankruptcy following the war, but they lost little time in devising a new method of accumulating money, that of working the ex-slaves under mortgages. What Miltiades Vaiden predicted in *The Forge* thus comes about, and ownership of land is shifted from the manor to the store. And, with the shift, the Negroes are still the losers. In his store, Handback makes a practice of short-weighting Negroes who work for him as sharecroppers. He justifies this practice by saying that the Negroes never discern the 10 percent he short-weights them and that it is not enough to hurt them anyway. If the money is no longer in planting, it is, Miltiades recognizes, "where it has always been — in niggers" (52).

The Negroes, too, recognize the realities of the changed economic situation; and, when Toussaint asks his mother if he should stand up for a whole pound of bacon at the store, she pragmatically answers that he should not. The scene that ensues is remarkable in that it brings into focus much of the complexity of the social structure in the South. Miltiades, then a clerk in Handback's store, waits on Toussaint and does give him a full pound of bacon. The Negro, however, questions the weight and is literally kicked out of the store by Miltiades. The irony here is characteristic of Stribling: Toussaint, expecting to get cheated, did not, and thus brought on a manhandling from his own father (unknown, of course, to both the man and the boy). Miltiades gives Negroes a full pound not out of any sense of integrity or sympathy; he does so simply to insure that, when he gets his own store, the Negroes will trade with him. Although, as in many a case in Stribling's work, coincidence is exploited in the scene, the result is dramatic as well as ironic — showing the conflict between an inner desire of a man to reach a goal and the forces that his environment pits against him. Miltiades, on the one hand, dreams of gaining affluence and making his life worthwhile by recapturing what he lost when Drusilla Lacefield (in *The Forge*) deserted him and when the war subsequently destroyed the Old South. Toussaint, on the other hand, strives to make more of his life than the social forces in the South will permit.

For Miltiades, his return to the land as an overseer for J. Handback, provides him with an awareness of how the "other half" lives — the Negroes and poor whites who did not move to Florence after the war. Among both groups he perceives a combination of ignorance, lassitude, and indifference as he attempts to convince them of the importance of fertilization and crop rotation. Staring over the jaded fields that have been planted decade after decade with cotton, Miltiades thinks of all the tenant farmers who "were like weeds which sprang up on the thin soil and died down in swift generations" (108). No matter how much they produce, they can never do better than break even. Miltiades also realizes that, in addition to being cheated, many of the white tenants are being steadily replaced by Negroes on the land because the latter are more easily duped by the landlord.

While Stribling graphically points out the plight of both Negro and white tenant farmers resulting from their forced dealings with men like J. Handback, he makes no effort to castigate these economic exploiters of land and people. On the contrary, his argument is that such men were necessary in the early steps of the development of a New South. Without them, the land would have produced nothing, and the entire section would have fallen still deeper into poverty.

It is perhaps symbolically fitting that Miltiades Vaiden's new start in life coincides with the election of Grover Cleveland to the White House. Cleveland's election is seen as a new chance for the South by the whites but as a dire threat by the Negroes. If a Republican president set them free, the Negroes, in their naiveté, can only think that a Democratic executive would cast them back into chains. Such logic, however, is lost on Miltiades and others like him. He has a fixed concept of Negroes that renders him totally incapable of understanding their feelings and behavior. He can only feel anger and frustration that they were ever set free.

Especially does Miltiades fail to understand the quadroon Gracie as a person. In *The Forge*, he used her body; in *The Store*, he uses her loyalty to hide the money he receives from the stolen Handback cotton. That her conscience bothers her about the stolen money, however, amuses Miltiades. He cannot comprehend that having hidden money stolen from Handback, she can no longer live in the cottage the merchant has been providing her. When she gives her savings, intended for Toussaint's education, to help Handback in his bankruptcy, Miltiades discounts the gesture as nothing more than an example of Negro foolishness. Moreover, he discourages her aspirations for Toussaint's getting an education by pointing out that an educated Negro has no place in the social structure of the South.

Gracie is unquestionably one of Stribling's best-drawn characters. In neither *The Forge* nor *The Store* does she play a dominant role;

yet she emerges in both novels as a woman of considerable dimen-
sion. Herself a product of miscegenation and raped by her own half-
brother and bearing his child, she is a connecting link between the
white and black races. Like Dilsey in William Faulkner's *The Sound
and the Fury*, she has a strength and an understanding that surpasses
that of the white characters in the novels. Ironically, the only person
who recognizes these qualities in Gracie is J. Handback, who, when
he learns that Gracie hid Miltiades' stolen money, takes his own life
without ever realizing that it was not losing the money but being
betrayed by Gracie, whom he loves, that destroyed his will to live.

Gracie's primary concern in *The Store* is for her son Toussaint. She
wants for him what can be his only as a white person. She con-
templates moving to Mexico where she and Toussaint could escape
the stigma of being black; but Toussaint, with a mind of his own rejects any idea of passing for white and marries Lucy Lacefield, a
black girl. Gracie is again on the road to tragedy.

## II   *The Force of Love*

Stribling once said, "The will guesses, but it never guesses right."[2]
Such a comment describes Miltiades Vaiden's situation after he has
opened his own store (with J. Handback's money) — one like
thousands of other stores scattered over the South. His original plan
was to make only a temporary establishment on Courthouse Square
and later to build a more dignified store. But he has become trapped
in a financial maze of mortgages — so much so that his dream of a
fine business is vanishing because all of his money is tied up.
Miltiades is sensitive enough to realize that something is missing in
his life, but he is not sensitive enough to grasp just what it is. He is
not a patron of the arts, and he pursues none of the graces of life. He
is, in short, little better than Handback and the thousands of other
"money grubbers" in the South. Disturbed and disappointed with
what he has made of his life, he feels an obligation to do something
beautiful, to recapture the gentility of the Old South, where the
making of money was not an all-consuming passion. The beautiful
thing he decides to do is to build a huge manor house that will em-
body within itself all that was once fine and gracious in southern life.
Though Drusilla Crowninshield refuses to share Miltiades' dream as
his wife, because she realizes that she has never been anything other
than a symbol to him, her daughter Sydna, impressionable young
girl that she is, agrees to marry him and to rest "in the embrace of
that romantic figure, who on the battlefield of Shiloh had promised
her dying father to care for his little daughter" (422).

Thus, in this novel, Stribling juxtaposes two marriages — Sydna Crowninshield's to Miltiades Vaiden and Lucy Lacefield's to Toussaint Vaiden (the Negroes' parents had taken the names of their respective owners). Ironically, then, the Vaidens and Lacefields, never able to come together in *The Forge*, have done so, at least figuratively, twice in *The Store*. A conversation that Miltiades has with the mystic Landers indicates that Stribling had more in mind than merely irony or coincidence in bringing the two couples together. When Miltiades asserts that love is based on the giving of sex, Landers argues that sex reactions are too much alike to be the basis of love. A man does not want any woman — just one; and, for that one, he will wait and deny himself. Such a situation suggests to Landers that "love is directed by spirits who are not yet born. They use matter to frame a universe for themselves; just as the first effort of life in the scum of a pond is to frame a universe for itself" (494). For Landers, then, "the force that matter feels when it is being drawn to serve life is love" (495). Possessed of his hard-shell Baptist father's disdain for anything mystical, Miltiades cannot grasp what Landers means. He is not truly in love with Sydna; she is to be merely an ornament in his beautiful manor, "an angel, remaining on earth to remind us there was once an Eden" (467). Miltiades' lyrical expression here seems more rehearsed than spontaneous. If Landers's vision is directed to the future, Miltiades' vision is riveted to the past and can be expressed only in clichés, the very nature of which robs him of any genuine expression of feeling.

In the attraction between Toussaint and Lucy, however, there seems to be a positive force. They represent a new breed of Negro; and their view, unlike the colonel's, is toward the future; and neither is willing to remain subservient to white people. Toussaint shows this early in the novel when he refuses to run when two white boys throw stones at him and again when he is determined to stand up for a whole pound of bacon. Lucy refuses Miltiades' offer to keep house for him and Sydna, for neither she nor Toussaint wants to go into domestic service. The colonel is astounded at such a statement because he cannot conceive of Negroes as anything more than servants. He describes Toussaint and Lucy to Sydna as "those new uncomfortable colored people who are springing up in the place of the good old-fashioned nigger" (467).

Nor can Gracie understand Toussaint, the son for whom she has the deepest affection and the greatest willingness to sacrifice. She recognizes that, in one sense, Toussaint does not belong in either white or black society and, in another sense, that, symbolically at least, he does not even belong to her, since her body had been merely a substitute for that of Drusilla Lacefield, whom Miltiades had expected to embrace that very evening (in *The Forge*). Thus, her relationship with her son is one of consistent hopelessness, of frustration, and of a lack of communication with him. Because he is whiter than she, she cannot interpret for him; his reactions are different from hers, and he cannot make the adjustments to society that she has. Also, his real father thinks that another man is his father. To his actual parents, then, Toussaint is subconsciously an orphan; to society, he is an outcast. Nor does Stribling provide us with any glimmer of hope for him. The only possibility for Toussaint is that, like Huck Finn, he strike out for new territory. But with Hardy-like certainty, fate, in the form of mother, money, or wife intervenes repeatedly to keep him at home and to lead him to his tragic end.

Lucy — an example of the educated, aggressive, modern Negro — marries Toussaint not because of his whiteness, as Gracie suspects, but because he does not bow his head to white people. Unlike Gracie, who accepts the tyranny of white people because she knows that resistance can end only in defeat, Lucy believes that the Negro should strive forward to a place of dignity and respect among all people. She encourages Toussaint to stand up to the poor white Alex Cady in a dispute over a wagon — the incident which ultimately leads to the lynching of Toussaint. Lucy is another wife, among many in history, who drives her husband to reach her ideals and in so doing aids in bringing about his destruction.

### III   *A Spiritual Death*

The last person who has a claim on *The Store* as his story is Jerry Catlin. He is largely removed from the major dramatic incidents in the novel, unless we consider his unsuccessful love affair with Sydna Crowninshield as a major incident. Yet Jerry, somewhat like the mystic Landers, hovers on the fringes of the story as a kind of observer, serving as a counter to the established religion of most Florentines and most southerners of the time. So concisely established is this religion that it is taken quite for granted. To Miltiades and the typical southerner, religion is explained in terms of the sun, the moon, people, animals, and above all the Bible. It is so simple to them that they cannot even talk about it but merely state it. Even when they want to, they cannot get an intellectual hold on its smooth sides.

Jerry Catlin is a self-proclaimed atheist who reads Ingersol and brazenly defies the existence of God by asking God to strike him dead as proof of His existence. On the other hand, he objects to attending chapel at college because his classmates and teachers are not sincere about it. He is fascinated by the occult and sees himself as someday being selected as an adept (a group of holy men who travel around the world doing good). Yet when he is given the opportunity on two occasions to do good, he does not accept it. He refuses to give Loob Snipes, a Negro, any of the food prepared for the watchers of the dead Ponny Vaiden; and he refuses to help Landers get Toussaint away from the jail just prior to the lynching. Negroes are out of Jerry's sphere of concern, except on an occasion such as his seduction of the Negro girl Pammy Lee. He is a product of the South and southern thinking; he cannot escape that fact. The most he can do in any positive way is to fumble around seeking for an answer. He does not find it in *The Store*. Thus the stage is set for his more significant role in *The Unfinished Cathedral*.

The lives of the main characters in *The Store*, as well as the life of the town of Florence, show the great social and economic disorganization that took place in the South as the result of the Civil War. From a highly structured antebellum society, the South during Reconstruction was turned inside out, both socially and economically. Miltiades at the opening of *The Store* might well symbolize the whole South. His dreams were shattered by the war and its aftermath, and he must find a new mooring for his life. Many of the old ideals and values are still very much a part of his makeup, but they must be redefined in light of the new forces operating on the South. The ingredients that will combine to make up the New South are basically the same as those that made up the Old South — Negroes, poor whites, the striving middle class, what is left of the aristocrats, and cotton. Before the New South can be realized, however, there must be a period of flux; and it is this period that *The Store* covers.

The South may look to the election of Cleveland to solve its problems; but when Cleveland wins and the Democrats are again in political power, the South finds that its problems are not magically solved. The presence of the Negro causes the greatest concern to southerners. The poor whites see him as an economic competitor; higher-class whites see him as a political threat; and all see him as a general threat to white supremacy. The effect on the Negro, as the tragedy of Toussaint shows, is often shattering. The Negroes do not have the power to do anything to prevent the whites from using and exploiting them. If the Cleveland administration is not the panacea the white South hoped for, neither has freedom been quite the panacea that the Negroes of *The Forge* hoped for.

Each of the major characters in *The Store*, except Gracie, struggles against his own personal social disorganization. Miltiades, while an overseer on the Lacefield plantation before the war, was pursuing a definite goal of success — eventually to own the plantation J. Handback, as we have seen, also had a goal in life. But neither has any control over the forces that operate to prevent him from reaching his goal. Whereas Miltiades is able to reorient himself and find a new purpose, Handback is not, and he commits suicide. The situation of Toussaint is even more complicated, since he exists in the no-man's-land between the Negro and the white. There is no possibility of self-realization for him in the South — not in the 1880s at least; yet his makeup forces him to go against accepted restrictions placed on Negroes, and he is destroyed. Jerry Catlin is caught between the predestination of his Vaiden ancestors and the spiritualism of a Landers. But unlike Landers, he cannot break away from his materialistic background and lose himself in the universal. His story, however, is merely begun in *The Store*.

Gracie is the only one of the main characters who seems to be aware of the conditions under which she must live her life. She has a strength that, while not oriented toward any specific materialistic goal, unless it be that of a better life for her son Toussaint, enables her to live with integrity, making her the one really likeable character in the novel. She is able to bring out what is probably the one true feeling that J. Handback has ever had — a love for her — though, ironically, he is unable to recognize it. Gracie's actions in the novel seem to illustrate the theory that Stribling developed in *Birthright:* that women are the ones who consistently place a higher value on love in matters that men often see only in a materialistic light. Sydna, too, might be seen in this way, though as a character she is less well drawn than Gracie. She is able to stimulate in Miltiades and in Jerry their better natures. Even if Miltiades sees her only as an ornament, at least this view is better than the crass materialistic view he had of Ponny when he married her in *The Forge*.

The South of *The Store* has come a considerable way from what it was in *The Forge*. Whatever validity the southern tradition had in antebellum days is gone now. The South has all but shrouded itself in a cloud of materialism, and the Negroes who wail in mourning over the death of the spiritualist Landers might well be wailing for the spiritual death of the South.

Perhaps because the South of the 1880s is more readily brought into focus than the South of the war and its immediate aftermath, *The Store* in terms of its overall structure stands as a more unified work than *The Forge*. Stribling, moreover, in the second novel of the trilogy draws his characters with a sharper definition than he did in the first. These aspects of structure and characterization combine to make *The Store*, on the levels of both fictional art and cultural history, a more effective work than *The Forge*.

## CHAPTER 8

# The Last Sacrament

RECIEVING a generally positive reception by reviewers, *The Store* went through five large printings during the first year after its publication and was a selection of the Literary Guild. The culmination of its popularity came on May 3, 1933, when it received the Pulitzer Prize for fiction "because of its sustained interest, and because of the convincing and comprehensive picture it presents of the life in an inland Southern community during the middle 1880's."[1] The road from Stribling's father's general store, where as a child he hid under the counter to write his stories, to the honor of a prize-winning novel may have seemed long for him; but he could finally say with some authority that he was indeed able to make a living writing. And he immediately began work on the last novel of the trilogy, *The Unfinished Cathedral*, which, though begun in New York, was completed in the seclusion of Clifton in the fall of 1933.

## I  *A Place Without Leisure*

Over thirty-five years and a world war separate the Florence, Alabama, of *The Store* from that of *The Unfinished Cathedral*. The time is the early 1920s, and the town is in the midst of a boom period brought on by the new government dam on the Tennessee River. The commercialism for which the Old South had so arrogantly ridiculed the North has now sprung up in Florence with a vitality that not too many years before would have been as unbelievable as the theory that Negroes were equal to whites. The conversations among land speculators and various business men on the trains coming into Florence reveal a South quite different from the one that Emory Crowninshield so confidently described to Marcia Vaiden in *The Forge*. These men talk not of beauty, courtesy, and graceful living, but of new apartment houses, golf courses, and industrial complexes.

Now in his nineties and a wealthy banker, Miltiades Vaiden is completely dominated by this new force of materialism. During his earlier life, materialism had always played a significant role in his activities, but it was tempered somewhat by the nebulous ideal that drifted on the fringes of his consciousness. Always a close observer of life around him, he learned after the Civil War that to succeed financially and socially, one had to adapt his methods to the prevailing conditions. By being flexible and not too virtuous, he has been able to exert considerable control over his changing environment. In his old age, he still accepts things as they are. Unlike his wife Sydna, he holds no illusions about the modern South and what is left of the old traditions.

When Bodine, the organizer of a secret society to stamp out Jews, Negroes, and Catholics, asks him why he doesn't consider the South his country, the old colonel responds that he considers the South simply as the place where he lives, a place that bears no resemblance to the ideal South that one side of him still yearns for. He cannot understand why Negroes were ever freed to run loose like stud horses and blames Yankee sentimentality for the whole situation. Ironically, Miltiades himself is instrumental in preventing the lynching of six Negroes, who are accused of raping a white girl. His motivation, however, is not compassion but the fear that the publicity from such an action will prove detrimental to the boom.

Stribling does not present Miltiades as simply a complete scoundrel or as an immoral man; morals and ethics are purely relative concepts to the colonel. He is honest when it is profitable to be honest or when his code of the southern gentleman requires it (usually on occasions not pertinent to his economic situation). To him, a business man should be as trustworthy as his business will allow and no more. He bases his life on the completely pragmatic philosophy that a man deserves what he gets if he can use it. As he tells Jerry Catlin, it is "not how you get a thing, it's what you do with it."[2] This statement is a recasting of what he tells Sydna in *The Store* when he speaks of wanting to do something constructive with the money he got from the stolen Handback cotton. Only now it sounds a little more crass and a little less idealistic. The "great" thing that he intends to do in *The Unfinished Cathedral* is to build a cathedral, complete with a crypt to "house his bones," as a monument to himself and the ideal that he has never been able to realize. This ironic goal becomes pathetic when the colonel, disappointed over his daughter Marsan's choice of a husband, makes light of him because he wants to work in a research laboratory. Miltiades cannot conceive of a man who would spend his life searching for facts that he did not intend to use for some personal profit.

The cathedral and his daughter Marsan are the only really important things in Miltiades' life. The dominant image that he holds of his daughter is "as a sweet innocent flower, a bluebell, who, one distant day, would kneel by his tomb in this cathedral and lift his name to God on the incense of her love and purity" (81). But, as Stribling indicates on several occasions, Marsan is not a stereotype of the traditional southern woman; she represents a new generation. Her mind, though it may at times turn back to the romance and grandeur of the Old South, is questioning and forward looking. She has no interest in her mother's elaborate and expensive efforts at tracing the Lacefield genealogy.

The old religious clichés, moreover, have little meaning for her; and she searches for a new reference. She thinks of her various aunts and uncles with their clear-cut sins and virtues, and she longs for the comfort of knowing sin from virtue without confusion. It seems to her that "back in the days of her father's youth, the very sins of the people were tonic experiences illustrating evil and promoting virtue, but nowadays who knew which was which" (128)? When she meets her cousin Jerry Catlin — now the Reverend Jerry Catlin — the question of how necessary ministers are comes to her mind. She knows that her mother cannot answer the question and that her grandmother's wisdom "went far beyond it in a sort of backward direction" (30). As for her father, he probably would not believe that such a question could arise.

For her answers, she turns to her high-school science teacher, J. Adlee Petrie, whose mind has also grown beyond the narrow limits of the southern tradition in religion. Petrie, who once lost a teaching position in Tennessee because of his views about evolution, sees religion in a mechanistic way. He believes it "unfortunate that the morals, laws, and manners of the modern world are supposed to hang upon a false-true test of some old Hebrew myths" (34). To him, man is ruled by cause and effect, but the problem is the gap between feeling the effect and discovering the cause. Even finding out the cause is of little value because things do not happen twice in the same way, and even if they did, "the set of causes you have figured out are the effects of causes still more remote" (112). Thus, chance becomes even more mysterious and inscrutable.

Stribling was often accused by reviewers and critics of relying too much on coincidence in his plot structure — and not without some basis. Yet, when we look at the plots and characters of the trilogy, we can see a close relationship between them and the philosophy that Petrie expounds to Marsan. Miltiades, through all three novels (more so in the first two), ponders the chain of cause and effect as it has operated in his own life; but he is never able to come to any definitive conclusion, as is also true of Jerry Catlin. It is not that they have had no choices to make; it is just that they are unable to comprehend fully how the alternatives they are offered came to be. Both would reject the idea of fate, as something that does not fit in with their materialistic concept of life; yet, each has had an ideal glimmering somewhere within him that would deny this concept. The point is that all the incidents of a Stribling novel are tightly related: each bears on a following incident and in turn is borne upon by a preceding one.

These relationships are not, however, as simple as the previous statement might make them seem. The boom and lynching in *The Unfinished Cathedral*, for example, are more than the results of a government dam and six Negroes's bumming from the North to find work on the project. We saw beginnings of these incidents in *The Forge* in the frontier individualism and Protestant predestinarianism of Jimmie Vaiden, in the views held by almost all southerners that Negroes are not really human, and in the southern code regarding women. The threads are from the same spool; *The Unfinished Cathedral* merely picks them up and weaves additional patterns — in this case around Miltiades, Marsan, Petrie, and Jerry Catlin II.

## II   *Religion and Materialism*

Jerry Catlin, at the beginning of the novel, is returning to Florence; but he is a quite different Jerry Catlin from the one we met in *The Store:* he is now middle-aged and a minister in the Methodist Church South. Through the influence of Miltiades, he has just been appointed assistant minister of the Pine Street Methodist Church in Florence. Once having had hopes of becoming a mystic, he has now joined the ranks of orthodox churchmen in the South who preach a kind of social religion. It is fitting that on the train with Jerry is Petrie, who, as we have seen, preaches a kind of mechanization of religion. Both men are products of southern progress, and both will have much to do with what additional changes overtake the South.

Jerry, at the beginning of the story, does not seem to be completely aware of the status of religion in the South or of his relationship to it. He recognizes the importance that churches have put on raising money; but when Dr. Blankenship, his superior, with his tremendous enthusiasm about the All Souls Cathedral, sends him to the Tri-Cities Realtors meeting to solicit funds for the project, Jerry thinks of how much the doctor will be able to accomplish spiritually when the church is completed. But we can hardly conceive of Blankenship's ever being a real spiritual leader; his vision of the cathedral is that of a vast social center with everything from restaurants to a billiard room. Blankenship's automatic comment about the proposed edifice is that it is "designed to minister to the Body, Brain, and Soul" (84) — and in that order very likely.

Blankenship points out to Miltiades that unless churches are turned into communal centers, they will lose their congregations. The feeling of younger people toward God and eternity, he laments, "oscillates between a myth, a rumor, a loneliness, and a poem" (287). Belief in God, at one time generally and easily accepted, now is the exception. Blankenship, too, has adapted to the conditions of the world in which he lives. He, Jerry Catlin, and others like them can bring nothing to the church except a reflection of the rampant materialism of the business community. Their congregations, moreover, "don't know exactly what they believe anyway" (40). It is little wonder that the husky teenager Red McLaughlin can answer Marsan Vaiden's question as to what a town would be like without churches by telling her simply to go where there are no churches and look around.

Although members of Tri-City Realtors have no interest in religion or in churches, other than as they might affect real-estate values, Jerry, with his experience at raising money, is successful with them. Indeed, every church he has occupied has been a business enterprise within itself; for it is expected to return, over and above its operating expenses, a certain amount to the General Conference of the Methodist Church South. His comment that money given to good service would be returned tenfold to the giver gets no response from the realtors because they themselves deal in glittering promises. He does strike a responsive chord, however, when he points out that one great cathedral will eliminate the necessity of having land set aside in the various subdivisions for smaller individual churches.

As Jerry is leaving the realtors' meeting, he is approached by a shabby little man who asks the minister's advice about a problem he is having with his young son. The boy has an imaginary playmate named Luggy, and he refuses to heed his parents' admonitions not to mention the apparition's name any more. Jerry brushes off the man with the declaration that such a situation is not unusual and that the boy will get over it. When the man asks Jerry to join him in prayer for the boy, the minister agrees to do so not with any spiritual purpose, but for the psychological effect it might have on the boy. As he prays, he sadly contrasts his early dreams of becoming a messiah with the person that he really is. Later in the novel, when Jerry does talk with the boy and learns that Luggy (actually a Negro) has said that the white people had better move away from Carver's Lane, he walks "on, deeply amused at such a fantastic discovery. . . . Junior's invisible companion and mentor was a little negro ghost . . . spirit . . . illusion . . . whatever it was" (313).

This incident is interesting because it not only shows that Jerry has little if any faith in prayer as anything more than a psychological device, but also indicates that, even in a period dominated by materialism, some events cannot be explained in any other than supernatural terms. Jerry, however, even though supposedly a spiritual leader, rejects any explanation that is not mechanistic in essence. Stribling makes use of several such incidents in each book of the trilogy; and his purpose is not to induce in the reader a belief in supernatural events but to show that "these hints, these innuendoes, these eyes peering through accidental chinks from some unimaginable outer void, instead of filling us with hope, are dismaying to our souls. We decline even to consider such experiences, or, if we do accept them, we let them hang in a kind of mental void unconnected with either our philosophies or our lives."[3]

The All Souls Cathedral, as Blankenship envisions it, will have few "chinks" through which anything spiritual can peer. There is no innovation in the cathedral in that respect, however, for the present Pine Street Methodist Church presents an image of sterility and hopelessness, "as if a group of journeyman carpenters, without any blueprints at all, had done all they could think to do and then had gone away and left it" (86). The church has nothing aesthetic about it, and neither will the cathedral when it is finished. Both are symbolic of the lack of anything beautiful or spiritual about the religion that has derived from the predestinarianism of Jimmie Vaiden.

The organ music that Jerry hears Aurelia Swartout playing in the church on several occasions contrasts with the stark interior of the place. The beauty of the music transcends the intellect and probes the emotions.[4] That part of Jerry Catlin that has been dormant since his youth is momentarily reawakened on these occasions when the music creates a dramatic juxtaposition in Jerry's mind of his past life and the glorified vision of his hoped-for future.

At one point Jerry is listening to Aurelia play when Sydna Vaiden enters the church, and a triple juxtaposition of forces occurs: the force of a religion that has lost its spiritual essence and become materialistic; the aesthetic force of music; and the backward looking force of the southern tradition that lives on in Sydna and is manifest in her comment to Jerry that, having a minister in one's family adds a certain tone, "especially when we get the cathedral finished and it becomes an old building softened by time and full of memories" (90). Jerry recognizes that what Sydna holds to be central in life is the debilitating force of the past that has little place in the South of the 1920s. In *The Store*, Drusilla, Sydna's mother, recognizes the crass materialism of Miltiades for what it is. Stribling, in his usual ironic way, makes these forces comment upon each other. As harsh and unyielding as it was, old Jimmie Vaiden's religion seems to have had a bit more substance to it than that which we see in *The Unfinished Cathedral*.

### III   Gone Are the Days

If there has been a deterioration in religion through *The Store* and *The Unfinished Cathedral*, considerable deterioration in the southern code of chivalry and gentility and noblesse oblige has also occurred. The society of the antebellum South was fragmented by the Civil War, never to be reconstructed. The southern code, as a result, is left with no framework in which to fit. It has not entirely passed out of existence, but it has deteriorated into a mass of meaningless clichés. When we recall such aristocrats as Caruthers Lacefield and Emory Crowninshield *(The Forge)* and their views of the code, we become aware of the level to which it has fallen in this last novel of the trilogy. Stribling points out this deterioration in an incident that stems from Miltiades' intervention in the lynching. Marsan Vaiden and her high-school companion Red McLaughlin witness the efforts of the colonel. When a man shouts out that Miltiades was once a cotton thief, Red, with a false show of chivalry — because he himself was about to shout the same thing — strikes him. Marsan momentarily weakens (the only time she does so in the novel) and is drawn to Red by his action in her father's behalf. Her feeling toward the boy is reinforced when she discovers that he is a member of a secret society, and she thinks, "No wonder he had defended her when he belonged to a kind of knights of the round table sworn to protect Southern womanhood" (66). The irony of this situation, and of the whole state of the southern code, is apparent when, about an hour later, Red seduces Marsan "with the animal innocence of a bear" (72).

Again we have an illustration of the cause-and-effect chain with which Stribling conceived of his plots. Marsan becomes pregnant (from her encounter with Red) as a direct result of two facets of the southern tradition in action — the eagerness to lynch Negroes and the desire to protect an innocent flower of southern womanhood. The irony is furthered when her pregnancy is discovered by her mother and Jerry Catlin when she faints in the latter's arms at the unveiling of a statue on the battlefield at Shiloh. Another facet of the southern tradition has been added since the Civil War — the cult of the Lost Cause, the glorifying of the Confederate soldier. The speaker of the day is moved to speak in emotional tones of the great past of the South and of the battlefield monuments erected as "chalices for the preservation of that rich heritage" (272). But whatever is left of that "rich heritage" has played a dirty trick on Marsan, and she knows it.

Also at the Shiloh celebration, Miltiades hears that the governor of New Jersey has refused extradition of one of the suspected Negro rapists. Unaware of his daughter's condition, he angrily rants that the Yankee governor's decision "can be counted as nothing more than an assault upon the purity of Southern women . . . to harbor the venomous serpents that pollute their innocence" (277). The irony is complete.

The contrast between Marsan and the rest of her family is apparent when Miltiades finally learns of the girl's pregnancy. Sydna's first thought is for an abortion to prevent any scandal, but Marsan is not willing to give up the baby even though she admits that the whole thing is a "mess." She regards the incident with Red in a matter-of-fact way: she calls Red's protecting her a mere reaction and her surrendering to him another reaction. Such a view shocks Sydna, who asks whether Marsan thinks people are just machines and whether she believes in God. Marsan's answer is that some girls believe in God and some don't, but most of them just don't think about it at all.

Neither Miltiades nor Sydna is capable of grasping the daughter's views. The colonel's first impulse is to get a gun and go after the seducer; yet he knows that his southern code is not a part of Marsan's world: "It was as if the symmetrical, well-formed world which he had given into Marsan's care when she and her generation came into existence had shivered to pieces in his daughter's hands" (294). The "symmetrical, well-formed" world that Miltiades recalls, however, did not shiver to pieces in Marsan's hands; it was destroyed long before her birth — and the colonel himself, with the many other southerners like him, contributed to its destruction. But the tradition dies slowly, for the South of *The Unfinished Cathedral* is like a snake that cannot slough off its dead skin.

The past hangs heavy in this novel, and none of the characters realizes it more than Miltiades — especially when he learns from Gracie that one of the Negroes being charged with rape is the grandson of Toussaint and Lucy (his own great-grandson, as incredible as that seems). He is caught in the same chain of cause and effect that he was in *The Store* when he was unable to save Toussaint from being lynched. He ponders over the events that have occurred since his rape of Gracie (his half-sister) in his father's barn many years ago, and he seems to discern in his life "the cold maleficent direction of Nemesis. And a sudden dismaying conviction seized on the old man that his future lay under the shadow of the same unseen power which had shaped the mien and horror of his past" (182). In perhaps the only virtuous act of his whole life, he succeeds in saving his great-grandson, seemingly because of a sense of obligation to Gracie and his offspring. This deed is about as close to love as Miltiades can come. Even his professed love for Marsan has been based not on her as a daughter, but on what she symbolizes for the old man. He carries this view of her so far that he would have her bear her child out of wedlock in order that the Vaiden name can be carried on.

Marsan, however, has a mind of her own and marries Petrie, her teacher. More than anyone else, he understands the girl; and he knows her to be a person for whom convention has little meaning, yet who has exquisite taste. He knows that Red caught Marsan in a moment of weakness and forgives her for it. In the meeting in which the two declare their love for each other, Petrie talks about the human striving for beauty as an attempt to bring about physical and mental perfection in the progeny of mankind. Beauty, then, is seen simply in terms of efficiency.

If we combine Petrie's ideas with what Jerry Catlin says to Aurelia Swartout about the place of love between men and women, we can go far in explaining the significance Stribling attaches to sex in many of his works. In discouraging Aurelia from marrying Tony Vicelli, Jerry argues that one should not marry simply on the basis of convenience because both physical and spiritual love are part of the human races's attempt to improve itself.

The marriages that occur in the trilogy and in *Birthright* show Stribling's evolutionary theory in operation. In *Birthright*, Peter Siner marries Cissie Dildine because there is a vital force that draws them together. They are, in a sense, opposites: Peter is whiter than Cissie and has more education than she has, but she has a greater vitality and desire for living than does Peter. In *The Forge*, Marcia, with her Confederate background and her notions about the possibilities for noble actions in life, marries Jerry Catlin, a Union man who has seen the worst realities of life. Also in *The Forge*, Drusilla marries Crowninshield, and Miltiades marries Ponny. These two marriages, however, might be termed marriages of convenience, or at least spur-of-the-moment affairs. The latter brings forth no children, while the former produces Sydna, who is merely her mother over again. Thus, in *The Store*, when Miltiades marries Sydna, we have the match that was intended originally in *The Forge*. Even the "informal" marriage of Miltiades and Gracie in *The Forge* is illustrative,[5] as is that of Toussaint and Lucy in *The Store*. Finally, in *The Unfinished Cathedral*, we have the marriages of Marsan and Petrie and of Jerry and Aurelia. There is little point in trying to show in what ways the offspring of these marriages are, or will be, improvements over their parents; for, in Stribling's view, such a process must go on for generations. The marriages do, however, indicate that he has been working his theories into the fabric of his novels.

## IV  Tragedy, Resignation, and Hope

*The Unfinished Cathedral* ends with the marriage of Marsan and Petrie, the promotion of Jerry Catlin II to a large Birmingham church, and the death of Miltiades Vaiden, who is killed when his unfinished cathedral is bombed by an irate union laborer. The colonel has resolutely refused to hire white union workers instead of the Negroes he gets at very low wages; for, since "niggers earned every penny of my fortune, they are going to lay every marble block in my tomb" (331). The ingredients of tragedy, resignation, and hope, then, are present at the end of the novel.

For Miltiades, the cathedral was to be his one great contribution to posterity, the embodiment of his Holy Grail. But, ironically, it is a symbol of materialism: materialism has built it, and materialism has destroyed it. It does, in a mocking sense, serve as a tomb for the colonel. The cathedral will, of course, be rebuilt; yet, it will always be unfinished, because it will lack the spiritual necessity that has been the touchstone of man's faith through the centuries. Religion has become little more than an ethic of practicality.

Jerry Catlin sees the state of religion reflected in the Conference of the Methodist Church South. The preachers at the conference look like a group of farmers who have become business men — and a great many of them were farmers before their call to the cloth. But they are business men who represent the most heavily capitalized industry in Alabama — the Methodist Church South. Jerry's sample sermon preached at the conference, "If there be no God, the Christian attitude is best," is received by both ministers and laymen with praise and admiration — "The idea that a man could join Jerry's church and receive the great uplift of religion without any real belief in God" (375). The sermon secures a pastorate for Jerry in Birmingham where they "needed a practical financier for their endless good and necessary works" (383). Jerry again recalls his romantic youth when his desire was to be an evangel to all the world, but he now knows he has recovered from this romanticism.

We have the tragedy and the resignation — where is the hope? It rests in Marsan Petrie and the little flannel bundle she holds to her bosom as Colonel Miltiades Vaiden lies "fixed and immovable" beneath a Confederate battle flag. The old and the new, the past and the future — "A volume closed and placed on the shelf of history" (352).

## V   *End of the Trilogy*

"What will the people in Florence, Alabama, say about you now?" a friend asked Stribling upon publication of *The Unfinished Cathedral*. "They can't say anything," Stribling responded. "They said everything when they read the first two books."[6] The people of Florence may have said all there was to say after they had read *The Forge* and *The Store*, but their feeling was still running high enough for a group of Florentines to file a libel suit against Stribling. When word of it reached Stribling in New York, he offered to contribute five hundred dollars toward the bringing of the suit, if it were brought while *The Unfinished Cathedral* was still selling. The suit was dropped, but on May 25, 1934, there appeared in the *Florence Herald* a letter from Stribling:

And I would like just here to make a very small payment on a very large moral debt which I owe Florence, Alabama. As everyone sees I have lugged the Scottsboro trial into the courthouse at Florence when it did not happen there at all. But I have done far worse than that. My trilogy has been a survey, more or less, of the foibles and amusing social kinks of the whole South, from Civil War times to present. I have focused everything I found in Florence because that was the scene of my prolonged story. I am in the position of a very sad literary dog, indeed, which drags every bone to its kennel, and I know this has been uncomfortable to perfectly nice and charming people who live in that house.

Naturally I need not say here that nowhere in the South exists such concentration of moral and financial quirks as I have depicted in Florence. In exculpation I will say that nowhere in the world, in any family or group of people, do there exist two hours of such strain, suspense, dramatic accent, hesitation and final catastrophe as may be found in any two-hour show in the theatres.

As a matter of literal fact, Florence, Alabama, is one of the pleasantest places I have ever known, filled with the most mellow and delightful folk. The only reason I chose Florence for the scene of my trilogy was because it had an interesting and romantic past and physical loveliness and softness, which gave me precisely the anesthetic relief which my ruthless narrative required.

So, as has happened to many another maiden, Florence has been mistreated because of her loveliness.[7]

*The Unfinished Cathedral,* completing Stribling's ambitious trilogy of the South, reflects once more the author's ability to tell a story that keeps the reader's interest and his mastery of the ironic method that lets the truth of human nature prove self-damning without excessive authorial comment. In this novel, moreover, as in the two earlier books of the trilogy, Stribling illustrates that the problems in a change of order were not happening merely *to* the South but *in* the people of the South — that each southerner, black and white, felt a division within himself that reflected the larger division in the section. Starting with a chessboard arrangement of character types but not stopping there, he blends the attitudes of these types into living individuals; and the resulting power of emotion makes an impact that mere intellectualizing cannot reach.

## CHAPTER 9

# A Respite for the South

FOLLOWING the completion of his trilogy, Stribling turned away from the South for his next efforts in fiction to New York City, a locale he found to be more than promising for his ironic thrusts. Two novels resulted — *The Sound Wagon* (1935) and *These Bars of Flesh* (1938).

## I  Big City Politics

*The Sound Wagon* is the story of Henry Caridius, whose discoveries about the structure of American politics comprise a series of disillusionments. Unsuccessful as a lawyer, Caridius decides that the only alternative he has to provide an adequate living for himself is to enter politics; and he runs for Congress with the backing of the reform-oriented Independent Voters' Alliance. Arguing against graft, political corruption, favoritism, and high taxes, Caridius has little chance of getting elected until the very day of the election when Congressman Blanke, the incumbent, dies. Krauseman, a corrupt political boss who had been backing Blanke, offers to support Caridius, if the latter will agree to carry out the organization's promises to various people who had supported Blanke's campaign. For his part, Caridius is trapped in a network of conflicting motives: he is for reform, but he must support his family and maintain his position and respectability.

Cardius is a microcosm of the competition which, as Congressman Bing later explains, exists among members of Congress, each of whom is sent to get what he can for his own section. Congress, Bing says, is "a trading post where you swap off what your section doesn't want for something it does want. But lay off any fool idea that you are legislating for the country at large, there ain't no sich animal."[1] Immediately, however, the most efficient method of accomplishing the goals that Caridius has is through connivance with his avowed opposition. Stribling, in the very beginning, then, negates any possibility of really reforming government.

In Megapolis, any politician who seeks office on a reform ticket is given many reasons for not carrying out his reform. Caridius, along with others like him, is protected by his town's corrupt political machine, whose members carefully keep him in ignorance and divert his attention with unsurpassed rhetoric to some distant altruistic goal until he, too, becomes a part of the machine. The corrupt lawyer, Myerburg, points out that a political reaction is not brought about by corruption or injustice because people are used to that. What brings out the vote, he says, is "the drama of a solitary Saint George riding forth to slay the dragon of corruption. That's what moves people . . . good theater. And when he's elected, the show's over and they all go home. And of course they give the dragon a rest so he will be in shape for the next exhibition" (150). Myerburg is a pragmatist and a cynic who believes that human nature makes it impossible for political reform to work. Thus, there is no such thing as moral responsibility on the part of a politician.

For his part, Krauseman serves as a go-between for Joe Canarelli's rackets and for Merritt Littenham's huge financial interests. His power strikes fear into the hearts of all, including Caridius, who fails to realize the legal symbolism of the suit of empty armor, bearing a sword in its right gauntlet, which stands in the entrance of Krauseman's home. Krauseman's theory on winning elections is that they are won by "picking out principles that people will fall for" (60). Failure to vote enables fortunes like Littenham's to exist, contrary to popular opinion, for the good of the country. The real object of money to Krauseman is as a "tax which the people of a country pay to its strong men in exchange for their personal freedom. That is why the people can't use their votes to take the money back again. The whole arrangement would be cancelled and the people would fall into direct slavery again, just as Germany, Italy, and Russia have done" (61). Krauseman regards himself, then, as a protector of the "oligarchy of wealth in America"; and he rationalizes his ideas with such paraphrases as "the sanctity of contracts," and "inalienable property rights."

With his moral compulsions destroyed one after another by logic, Caridius advances to national office, where the destruction continues. He soon ceases to succumb to the stirring propaganda of elementary-school history books and realizes that the glory of America and its government rests on a number of illusions. And he slides easily into the pattern of congressional life. When, for example, he discovers that his mileage allowance, larger than his salary, will pay for his commuting daily from his home to Washington, he also discovers the aesthetic benefits of flying. Later, when he learns that his unused stationary allowance can be taken in cash, he opposes such action in principle and selects a gold cigarette case instead. When an office boy is caught stealing postage stamps, the new congressman twirls the gold case in his fingers while he denounces the boy's stealing. He also becomes accustomed to procedure in the House, where business is conducted in private conversations unrelated to the debate going on and where only the chairman and the congressional reporter listen to speeches.

Another complication for Caridius arises from his relationship with Mary Littenham, who becomes his valuable assistant. In addition to being a wealthy heiress, she is better informed on politics and other current issues than he. An attachment grows between the two as they work and commute together. Caridius finds this woman that he does not possess an urgently desired object of his life, for his firm opinion is that the unattained woman, whoever she is, is always more desirable than a wife. He cannot bear to hurt his wife by asking for a divorce; and Mary, who understands his predicament, agrees to become his mistress. Caridius regards this unsubsidized relationship as a perfectly respectable one, but he is shocked when a Japanese gentleman sees America's lack of legalized prostitution as an economic cause-and-effect relationship. Because America is prosperous and not overpopulated, there has been no need to make provision for "young men and indigent men and ill-mated men as a class" (153). If there were such a provision, he points out to Caridius, there would be no need for abduction of women into vice.

Another plot thread in *The Sound Wagon* — one which involves an inventor and his friend Rose — enables Stribling to satirize free enterprise, which, contrary to its avowed purpose, cripples individual initiative. An old schoolmate of Caridius's, Jim Essary, has invented a new form for explosives that he would like to sell to the War Department; however, since he is an employee of the Rumbourg-Nordensk Company, he must surrender all patent rights on anything he invents to them. Caridius, rather than attempting to change the patent laws, which Essary thinks should be abolished entirely, searches for a way for his friend to make money on the invention outside the law. When he recommends to the Military Affairs Committee that the War Department buy the patent, his recommen-

dation is followed; and the contracts are awarded to the Rumbourg-
Nordensk Company which is controlled by the Littenhams. Caridius
himself benefits directly through investments made for him by the
Westover Bank, which is also controlled by the Littenhams.

At the time Essary's financial situation should start to improve, a
new concern emerges when the racketeer Caranelli demands that
Littenham pay "protection" for his factory. When Littenham uses
his influence to bring in federal troops to guard the factory,
Caranelli finds, much to his dismay, that he cannot "buy" the
troops. Thus, in an overwhelming maze of corruption, there seems a
ray of hope; it offers small consolation, however, because the suspi-
cion lurks beneath the surface that the reason the federal troops cannot be bought is a matter of geography: Canarelli has not extended
his operations far enough.

Canarelli subsequently decides to back Caridius for a seat in the
Senate in opposition to Krauseman's organization. When the
problem of finding an issue that will bring the voters to the polls
arises, Myerburg insists that they must have an issue that will appeal
to the emotions rather than to the intelligence of the electorate
because most of them "must be shoved clear to the wall
economically or get tremendously excited over something before
they'll vote. You have got to heat up and boil over this great mutton-
suet vote of America if you stand any chance at all of getting
elected" (315). Meltofsky advises Caridius to find two issues for the
campaign — one to get the attention of the people, and then another
later to get their votes. The decision is that Caridius will attack
Littenham for failing to pay his income taxes and for selling military
secrets to foreign enemies. They are aware, of course, that Caridius
made a speech supporting this sale, but Myerburg assures him that
nobody ever reads the *Congressional Record.*

Because of his attacks on Littenham, Caridius faces Mary
Littenham with some trepidation. He is amazed, however, when she
tells him that her father is pleased at the attacks. In fact, she points
out, her father's candidates always attack him in order to gain the
confidence of the people, thereby saving Littenham money that he
would have to use to buy votes. Littenham, moreover, feels that
Caridius's idea about the war secrets will create a war scare and
bring a large munitions appropriation to his munitions factory.
Caridius, who exhibits a childlike amazement at the duplicity of the
activities of others, learns only slowly that the financier plays both
ends of the game at once and is certain to win in every instance. But

Littenham, in spite of his power, feels so insecure that he has constructed under a pool on his estate a secret retreat against the day when, as if he were some feudal baron, the vassals under him will rise up to destroy him. In the end, however, the machine that he has created continues to operate; and the murder of his daughter by members of the gang who are a part of that machine is one tragedy against which he can not fortify himself.

*The Sound Wagon* is a tightly constructed novel with its four plots which are developed largely through conversation. The mass of dialogue, as a result, distinguishes the physical appearance of the printed page from that of, for example, *Teeftallow* or *The Forge*. Through these dialogues, Stribling topples from their pedestals many of the revered misconceptions of the American people; for the ramifications of each plot reach into many phases of American life, including, among other things, a satire on the League of Women Voters, some of whose members want a federal appropriation to carve pictures on the mountains. In the major plot, with the ostensible goal of satirizing American politics, the writer utilizes the career of Henry Caridius to destroy the common misconception that an honest man with pure motives can get into, let alone remain in, office. Because the awarding of government contracts is necessary to big business, the Littenham interests support not the morally right (for there is no "right") but both parties. An important correlative is Littenham's ownership of rival newspapers: there is no "freedom of the press," strictly speaking, because the newspapers also find it necessary to make concessions. That the path to an ultimate good may be obstructed is a basic assumption; that there is no path, as well as no ultimate good, remains to be learned by people like Caridius.

Through the Canarelli plot, Stribling shows the hopeless web spun by the labor unions to entangle their innocent victims. Canarelli's conviction for illegal exportation of gold into Canada indicates that he had stepped out of his natural element in attempting to compete with Littenham. His success in browbeating the poor and the ignorant derives from his having been one of them; for, like the would-be dictators in *Fombombo* and Angelito in *Red Sand*, he lacks the innate qualities of good breeding which would enable him to compete with tycoons like Littenham.

The subplot involving Caridius's relationship with Mary Littenham satirizes American views on sex. Like Strawbridge in *Fombombo*, Caridius approves only of refined, controlled premarital or extramarital relationships. In other words, secrecy engages sanctity. His wife at the beginning of the story is an irrationally jealous termagant; that she emerges at the end of the novel to take her husband's place in politics serves as another example that necessity often uncovers hitherto untapped resources.

The subplot involving Jim Essary and his fiancée Rose shatters the myth of free enterprise. To profit from his own invention, Jim becomes a criminal by dodging a contract and by selling his invention to a foreign country. His death in a demonstration of his war machine is shrouded in mystery. Was it accidental or not? With such questions unsolved, the novel ends; and the impersonal forces of the universe, the reader feels, continue to function, unaltered by man's utmost but ineffectual exertions.

## II  *Mechanized Intellect*

*The Sound Wagon* was hardly off the press when Stribling began work on his next urban novel, *These Bars of Flesh;* he completed it toward the end of 1937, and it was published by Doubleday in 1938. Basically, the novel deals with the experiences of Barnett, a deposed gentleman politician from the South, who enrolls for the summer session at Megapolis University. At the university, Barnett enters a coldly mechanized world where even the most intimate emotions are exposed in unfeeling intellectualized conversations — a world in which he does not fit. Neither unfeeling nor intellectual himself, he nevertheless cheerfully makes the best of his predicament. While a member of the Georgia legislature, he had passed a law requiring county-school superintendents to have degrees; when he was defeated at the next election, he ran for the position of county-school superintendent and, pressed to the wall by his own law, attends a Megapolis summer session to acquire, if not a degree, at least a certificate. His innocence in the assumption that such a possibility might exist is no more farfetched than many of the regulations already in force at Megapolis. In fact, there are many requirements for students but few for professors.

The process of Barnett's orientation at Megapolis is greatly aided by a Miss Lester from Iowa, a student who cannot pass a course in speech because of a lisp but who has taken the required course so often she now teaches it. She provides Barnett with several kinds of practical information, beginning with "There is no use asking a professor about anything except something he teaches himthelf."[2] Barnett, obeying the southern code of chivalry, leaps to her defense

when a "yellow nigger" bumps her. The policeman who breaks up
the fight advises Barnett that one cannot start a fight just because
two people bump together; in Megapolis, it happens all the time.
The Negro's refusal to press charges requires no explanation; like
everyone else in Megapolis, he hasn't time.

Becoming accustomed to the rush and flow of humanity is in itself
a challenge to Mr. Barnett. Wherever something is made available
for one person, a multitude gathers. At Megapolis, if a person is not
sitting in class, he is usually standing in line or in a crowd, or he is
marching in a parade. When he discovers Mr. Schmalkin, a Russian,
following a parade protesting his own deportation (because
Schmalkin knows nothing of the deportation order), Barnett breaks
into laughter. Since no one knows anyone else in the North, he says,
public opinion must be expressed through some form of advertising
— parades, telegrams to Congress, radio, and causes. Causes are especially important because people find it easier to identify with a
cause than with an individual.

As a visitor from the South, Barnett never thinks far enough to
relate his observations to the philosophy which he hears expounded
at Megapolis, but it is purely a mechanistic philosophy, and the impersonal universe must be a reflection of the impersonal world of
Megapolis. The famed psychologist Dr. Fyke, who puts Barnett to
work arranging material for another of Fyke's books, attacks the
theistic concept of immortality. His method is to file innumerable
cards describing various persons and then to find whether one person, after death, relates the material on the secret card through his
medium, Miss Redeau. Barnett's friend Derekson explains that Dr.
Fyke is not trying to disprove anything; as a scientist, he is neutral.
Throughout the novel, however, Dr. Fyke makes it clear that he
himself does not believe in immortality; the experiment will serve
only to free other disillusioned persons. The Russian, Schmalkin,
who has witnessed much of the sacrifice of the individual for the
cause of the state, explains the consequences of proving the nonexistence of the soul by pointing out that all of modern civilization,
with its materialistic emphasis, would collapse if man were really immortal. Immortal beings would not permit themselves to be herded
into armies to murder each other.

Dr. Fyke's philosophy extends to ultimate, universal, cause-and-
effect relationships. He points out that, just as a patient deprived of
food in an experiment first loses ability to formulate new theories, so
international councils for preventing war, unable to find new ways to

keep the peace, enter a mental slump in which they seek the easiest solution to their problems, which is war. Another part of the problem of existence for the American people, says Dr. Fyke, is a nervous instability based on their concentration on money. Money is only significant in that it can be used to purchase future satisfactions, but choosing these satisfactions keeps man in a state of mental indecision. The pursuit of money, then, leads indirectly to nervous instability. Ironically, Dr. Fyke values his time at two hundred dollars a day, and his own pursuit of money is the reason he cannot afford to spend time writing his own books.

Although Dr. Fyke does not converse with Schmalkin, their comments in the area of spiritism are similar; they reach the same goal, the same realization, through different routes. The difference is that Fyke as a scientist merely explains; Schmalkin as a responsible citizen evaluates. Fyke also seeks the causes of materialism and maintains that organized religion has had a part in the formation of modern materialism: the medieval mind, he believes, would have accepted all supernatural phenomena as the work of spirits and gods, but modern religion sees all spirits as evil spirits. The result is a progressive slide into a materialism that rejects the functioning of the subconscious and directs its mental activities completely to mechanics.

All these thoughts provide Dr. Fyke with a title for a new book: *The Debt You Owe as a Materialist to Organized Religion.* The book, in keeping with Fyke's purpose of writing for the consumption of millions, must bear a title which will indicate that the individual, already in pursuit of material happiness, will be encouraged to continue his present course. As a scientist, Dr. Fyke must merely make observations; he must not suggest that a different objective might be more beneficial to society. Fyke's scientific nature is thereby freed of moral obligation.

In the society of Megapolis, Barnett listens to Schmalkin discuss the symbols of religion by relating them to those of superstition and the lack of spiritual power in mankind. When told that the southern Negro woman believes childbirth pain will be cut in two if a sharp axe has been placed under her bed, Schmalkin remarks that religion and superstition bring the spirit to the aid of the flesh in curing ills. Modern medicine, however, enables human beings to escape pain without spiritual effort and therefore militates against achieving greater spiritual strength. Thus, on the one hand, a materialistic society lacks the human compassion which a belief in immortality would necessitate; on the other, the comforts of modern medicine deprive man of the spiritual strength and growth which are the only qualities which distinguish him from lower forms of life.

A third analytic mind, that of Dean Overbrook, is required to extend the discussion of the symbol into another area — that of politics. Just as Schmalkin and Fyke indicate that the further a nation's people move away from religion, the less able they are to direct their own affairs, so the further a people move from the symbols of the individual in politics — "shirt sleeves, torn handkerchiefs, flop hats" — the more they remove themselves from the process of self-government. The dean explains that the further away a nation moves from a given social reality, the more it must rely on symbolism to give credence to that reality, until ultimately it develops a ritualism to provide the necessary dramatization of something that is no longer fact.

Within the university, a group of students is enthusiastic about communism; and their interest apparently springs from the impersonal forces surrounding them. Because they know few individuals, and because their adjustment to their world is nothing more than a battle of wits, their interest is in a cause rather than an individual. Stribling transposes this espousal of a cause into a very humorous incident in which a Miss Casings, a friend of Fargason Medway, who is Barnett's advisee, first learns the horror of Schmalkin's life history. That Schmalkin should have seen his sister burst open from starvation because the government was withholding wheat to gain an economic foothold in foreign trade impresses Miss Casings to the extent that she abruptly discontinues her relationship with Medway.

Medway then conceives the plan of going to another woman, in order, as he says, to protect his health. When he begins having several kinds of biological and psychological problems which force his removal to a hospital, Miss Casings, realizing the enormity of her deed, promises to return to their normal relationship, the only one based on logic. Medway's nervous instability is proved to be entirely responsible, however, for all his difficulty; he could fake all the symptoms for syphilis and actually believe he had it, until science, in the form of a Wassermann test, rescues him from his hospital bed. When Barnett last sees the two of them, they are marching in a parade to their wedding; and the parade banners protest the dismissal of Barnett for radicalism. When Barnett insists that he was actually fired for conservatism, Medway explains that the signs follow a principle of radicalism, that of seizing on any fact and shaping it for an attack against the capitalistic system. Once capitalism is replaced by communism, however, misstatements will no longer be permitted.

In the world people think they inhabit, they are not capable of deciding anything; everything must be decided for them by their leaders. If this system is applied everywhere, then the nature of a cause is disguised; and, negating Barnett's earlier observation, people who do not know each other will be denied even a morsel of participation in the events which shape their lives; they will not even know the cause for which they parade. That logic can never solve every human problem, as proved in the instance of Miss Casing's reconciliation with Medway, Medway fails to realize. He learns nothing from experience; and, by his own "logic," he denies himself the opportunity to prove that there may be human values which function independently of cold reason.

Occasionally some "uncertain illumination" passes through Mr. Barnett's mind, and he experiences a faint glimmer of the truth which Medway and others overlook. When Medway justifies the execution of about a third of the ranking officers in the Bolshevik army on the basis of the importance of political solidarity of a nation's people, Barnett vaguely realizes that, though on a lower level the advancement of society is more important than the individual, on a higher level the individual is the more important. Man, in the latter sense, is preparing himself not merely for a material existence but for a spiritual existence as well. Barnett lacks the loquaciousness, however, of his northern acquaintances; and, if he could put this thought into words, he would never be able to think and talk fast enough to gain or hold an audience.

The trait which distinguishes Megapolis University from the rest of Stribling's fictional world is its application of logic. At Megapolis, in the name of logic, requirements can be waived, standards removed, an argument advanced to prove or disprove any theory, and even the status quo continued because some analytic mind recognized that it now exists. A notable and humorous example is the work Barnett does for Dr. Fyke. Failing to arrange the newspaper clippings satisfactorily for Fyke to dictate a book from them, Barnett discovers that he can still gain academic credit for the project if he gets someone to do the task for him. The justification for allowing credit under such a circumstance is based on the logic that Barnett is working toward a degree to qualify him as a superintendent of schools and that if he can find someone capable enough to arrange Fyke's material, he will have sharpened his own adminstrative skill.

The application of logic to any pattern of thought can have both beneficial and adverse effects, and the impression is that the great minds of the university prefer that the emotional part of any decision not be recognized. If possible, where emotion exists, they would like to blend it with logic, as in the case of assigning Barnett a class in practical politics to teach. Since he does not know enough to begin learning anything, there is no course for him to take; but no one wants to discourage him entirely. He has had experience in politics, and certainly there is a need for a practical, not merely a theoretical, politics course. As a result Barnett becomes a lecturer.

In class, Barnett the politician parallels Caridius of *The Sound Wagon* in that he sees no reason for a man to enter politics except that the man is unsuccessful in some other endeavor. His removal from the chair of politics occurs because he disagrees with Dr. Nisson's talk in which the latter, newly appointed to service with the New Deal, states that the American people will be made happy by being paid for keeping his party in power. Having lost his position at the university, Barnett also learns that someone else has been given the superintendent's post that he has been preparing for. Meanwhile, though, the New Deal government, to insure the vote of the farmers, pledges a parity which will make raising cotton profitable. When Barnett then plans to return home to raise cotton, he unwittingly proves that Nisson was right.

The one consolation in this novel about the overwhelming effects of applied science is that, where science condemns, it can also save. In the case of Fargason Medway, where the individual seeks to mislead himself and others, indifferent science can establish truth. In a scientific invention, also, Schmalkin sees the hope for reestablishment of humanistic principles. One of the inventors of television, Schmalkin has hopes that this medium of communication, because it will put before the eyes of man all the suffering and tragedy in the world, might make man more compassionate. Schmalkin never realizes that material may not be televised at random — that effective selection and concentration of subject matter could reduce even his hope to a bare minimum.

This novel, the second of Stribling's satires, has several other parallels with *The Sound Wagon*. The newspapers which were prone to misstatement in *The Sound Wagon* reappear in *These Bars of Flesh*. The inventor's problems with being unable to profit from his own invention reappear in Schmalkin; in this case, the university is automatically the owner of Schmalkin's television. The emotionalism of the voters in *The Sound Wagon* is transferred in *These Bars of Flesh* to students who do not know why they are parading but who parade for any "radical" cause. The comments of Dr. Snell, Mary Littenham's politics professor in *The Sound Wagon*, reappear in *These Bars of Flesh* but are much elaborated upon by Dean Overbrook and by Dr. Nisson. Barnett himself does not theorize about politics; as a politician from the South, he more closely resembles Congressman Bing of *The Sound Wagon* than any other character.

*These Bars of Flesh* deals in passing with many other aspects of university life: the professor who corrects his wife's grammar and whose son is a genius; the fact that assistant professors do not earn enough money for man and wife to go out together (she hasn't a proper dress); the stressing of the difference in rank (Stahl isn't a professor, he's an assistant professor"); and the belief that any thought passing through Fyke's great mind is worth publicity. The only person who transcends "these bars of flesh" is the French woman medium, Miss Redeau, whose fleshly attraction cannot be denied and through whom the spirits of departed persons speak. Under Dr. Fyke's tutelage, however, she attaches no significance to her clairaudiency.

As examples of Stribling's ability to turn to new settings, *The Sound Wagon* and *These Bars of Flesh* are interesting enough. More than that, however, they show his skill as a satirist. Blending humor and intellectual content with satire, Stribling in these novels emphasizes again, and perhaps more cogently, his ideas of the destructive effect of materialism on American society. In this sense, though they lack the dramatic impact of the trilogy, *The Sound Wagon* and *These Bars of Flesh* stand as significantly successful ficitional efforts.

## CHAPTER 10

# Through This Dust
# These Hills Have Spoken[1]

T HE Florence, Alabama, Yacht Club — an imposing white pil-
lared structure facing the Tennessee River just above the Wilson
Dam — stands as a testament to the economic progress that Florence
has made since the turn of the century and to the spirit of gentility
that can still be found in such southern towns. On January 21, 1964,
under a blue sky and a brilliant springlike sun, the Yacht Club was
particularly picturesque when over a hundred members of the
Florence Woman's Club gathered there for a luncheon meeting — a
meeting that might well be marked as one of the more interesting
minor ironies in southern literary history. The speaker for the
meeting was the then eighty-two-year-old novelist Thomas Sigismund Stribling, who some thirty years before had aroused the ire of
Florentines for his candid treatment of the town and its people in his
trilogy of the South — *The Forge, The Store,* and *The Unfinished
Cathedral.*

Time, however, erases much; and the ladies at the Yacht Club that
January day were enthusiastic in their appreciation of Stribling's
humorous talk and in their requests for autographs. So, too, were the
college students who had overflowed the auditorium of Florence
State College two weeks before to see and hear the novelist in his
first formal appearance in Florence since the publication of the
trilogy. Under the headline "Stribling Warmly Greeted at Talk," the
story in the *Florence Times* opened with the following two
sentences: "T. S. Stribling returned to Florence Thursday, teased an
audience with humorous remarks and received a very warm reception thirty-two years after his prize-winning novel shocked local
residents. The Pulitzer Prize winner spoke to an overflow crowd at
Kilby Auditorium as a guest of the Florence State Convocations
Committee and was surrounded by students who obtained his

108

autograph on slips of paper, notebooks, and paperback copies of *The Store*."[2]

Tom Stribling had finally come home. But more than that, he had come full circle — from unknown writer of Sunday-school fiction to Pulitzer Prize winner to an almost forgotten man of letters. For, after *The Sound Wagon*, Stribling's career as a novelist was over. He wrote several novels subsequently, but none of them ever reached publication. From then on, his published creative efforts were in the area of short fiction for such magazines as *The Saturday Evening Post* and *Ellery Queen*. He returned in 1959 to live permanently in Clifton, now a quiet, unobtrusive cluster of houses and stores that, were it not for the modern automobiles parked here and there and the television antennae scattered among the rooftops, would belie the twentieth century. Actually, he had always returned home regularly through the years and, indeed, did much of his writing there; for Clifton's "quiet soothed my frayed nerves and its reality restored my sense of balance. Here were the old familiar things — four-square and actual — things I could touch — reawakening the imagination and mood of youth."[3] And there, in the hills he loved so well, he passed his last years, dying of cancer on July 10, 1965.

## I   *Literary Vision*

Turning his back on the fundamentalism of the Tennessee hill country, T. S. Stribling accepted the determinism of the nineteenth-century scientists; and all of his novels reflect an artistic strategy based on that rejection and acceptance. From the drama apparent in the everyday lives of the people around him, Stribling drew his raw material and set his novels in particular times and places; for he believed that people, after all, are merely products of the time and place in which they live. Miltiades Vaiden, for example, is what he is because of the external forces that impinge upon him. In *The Forge*, prior to the actual outbreak of the Civil War, his dream is to succeed materially within the framework of the antebellum South. By the end of the novel, however, he realizes that prevalent economic and political conditions have destroyed the traditional South and that he must adopt a new means to achieve success. The same can be said about Peter Siner in *Birthright*: intellectually, he is not the same as he was before he went away to college; but, physically, he is; and in the South, it is his physical appearance that is overriding. The external forces that are exerted on him in Hooker's Bend preclude any possible fulfillment of his dream. And so it goes, through many

characters in Stribling's novels — Abner Teeftallow, Parilee
Pomeroy, Jimmie Vaiden, Railroad Jones, Henry Caridius, to name a
few.

The people mentioned above may not be able to unravel the
mysteries of the universe; but, within the bounds of social convention, they work toward their sometimes nebulous goals. The
successful are those who are flexible enough to maneuver within a
world of changing conditions. As Stribling once said in an interview,
regarding change in the world,

> every society in every day of its existence is continually changing — and it is
> not changing according to any one man's conception. It isn't a logical
> change; it's a biological change. And that goes on, and the logical concept
> pursues this biological change and makes different futures that men think
> the biological change will pursue. But it never pursues the one that they
> think. For instance, you take the Communists today. For them to imagine
> that society will pursue the Communistic theory and continue on it is perfect
> nonsense, because you can't plan out what is going to become of a society.
> They follow it in some degree for awhile, and then there will be com-
> promises and different changes, and it will never come out by possible
> means the way that the planners planned it. So, any plan that is cut and
> dried for any society will never be realized.
>
> You take our democracy. We were going to be democratic with
> everybody. Everyone would have a vote and influence in the society. We
> break up into crime syndicates; labor unions who are users of force and users
> of the crime syndicates; and capitalists who own everything and who are op-
> posed to labor unions and crime syndicates, yet use the labor unions and
> crime syndicates when necessary. So, it's always an interchange of opposing
> factors, and nobody can say that democracy means a certain thing. It can
> never be accomplished or carried out with any coherent plan. It's always
> breaking this way and that through a biological process — never a logical
> process.[6]

In Stribling's novels, then, geographical setting is of vital
significance not merely as local color (since he did not divorce his
stories from the mainstream of American life by making them seem
special or esoteric) but as a force that prescribes a whole way of life.
This observation is true whether the novel in question is set in the
South, in New York, or in Venezuela. Stribling was concerned with a
particular vision of man in a given locale at a given period in history.
As a result, his novels fall into the classification of realism. Moreover,
because his novels treat the social institutions in question with a
documentary bias, some critics and reviewers have accused the

novelist of propagandizing for social reform and have seen his thesis as dominating all other elements in his work.

In talking about propaganda in literature, Stribling himself, on one occasion, said, "Now it has been my experience that the man who writes realistically need never trouble himself about raising the issue of propaganda. . . . the persons he writes about will do that for him."[7] On the same occasion, he elaborated on his view of the relationship of propaganda to literature:

Propaganda, the spreading of ideas by emotion mixed or unmixed with reason, is the only instrument that will move a democracy. And the more completely democratic any country becomes the more completely will it depend upon propaganda. I am speaking now not as an idealist looking forward to a millennium of an educated citizenry, but as a realist looking to the here and now.

So the only practical question that remains to be discussed is how shall propaganda be used.

It seems to me the only guide here is the artist's sincerity. This is almost self-regulating because unless an artist is sincere his propagandizing is false and for the most part useless. The people of a country are like schoolchildren; they do not fully understand their teachers but they know whether or not they are sincere.

If this reasoning be true, it converts the whole field of art into an honorable field for propaganda. Because no artist can depict any scene or passion without at least a conscious or an unconscious taking sides.

Therefore I say let all sects and creeds enter the lists. Let them dramatize their vision of life with whatever gifts they possess. If we cannot completely persuade each other, perhaps we can educate each other in some degree. And the people who listen and look, with their multitudinous instinct for selection, will choose whatever and whoever moves them with the most sincerity. The result is in the hands of that God who made all of us to think a little and feel a great deal.[8]

The documentary bias in Stribling's novels has as its motive, not the desire to change society, but the author's idea of an evolutionary process at work in life. Implicit in all of his major work is the Spencerian definition of life as the continuous adjustment of internal to external relations. From this view of life comes the corollary that evolution explains the origin of moral codes in the social struggle. Thus, a right action is one that leads to survival, and everything becomes relative. The question "what is man" is answered with the theory that man is whatever his time and place allow him to be.

In Stribling's vision, man is insignificant in the overall scheme of things; he is merely one result of the vast evolutionary process. Stribling's interest in character, therefore, did not lie in the same direction as that of Faulkner and others like the Mississippian. The dark recesses of an individual man's soul did not interest Stribling; what did concern him was whatever he could discern about man through objective observation. For only in this way can one, in the split second of eternity that he is on earth, see any instances of the evolutionary process at work. Stribling was interested in the "why" as well as the "what" of man's actions but only insofar as the "why" could be ascertained objectively. None of his characters, therefore, are neurotic or psychotic — a fact that, given the recent trend of fiction and criticism, has hurt rather than helped Stribling's reputation.

## II  *Literary Achievement*

Because Stribling set his novels in a given time and place and examined the existing way of life, it is perhaps easy for some to view them, at least on the surface, merely as social documents intent on bringing about change. But an analysis of Stribling's literary vision and of the novels it produced should make it clear that his intentions were not those of either a propagandist or a social reformer. His novels are not so much a search for an ultimate ethical or moral truth in life as they are an effort to show that time and change are the only enduring realities. Henry Belshue in *Teeftallow*, for example, sits in his shop and hears the many tickings of the clocks on the shelves, like "the flight of numberless tiny feet . . . as if Time might be a Lilliputian army double-quicking (to what purpose?) down the endless slope of eternity."[10] But, as "to what purpose", Stribling never fully answered the question. He was content to picture the world in mechanistic terms and to show its steady progression away from the spiritual to the material. We have this idea illustrated in the trilogy with the social and economic change that overtakes the South and the accompanying spiritual decline of religion. In this case, Stribling made of the South a microcosm of the world.

While, on the surface, Stribling's mechanistic views seem to rob man of all those qualities with which civilization has sought to endow him, we cannot dismiss the Tennessean's view or his work as being purely pessimistic. There seems to be a kind of optimism, for instance, in his celebrations of sex. Stribling emphasizes sex as a vital part of the evolutionary process; and the human concept of romantic love is a reflection of this vitality. Although this view of sex has already been discussed as it relates to specific novels, we might recall that four novels — *Birthright, Teeftallow, Bright Metal,* and *The Unfinished Cathedral* — contain a scene near the end or at the end of each novel in which a baby is either present or is in the thoughts of a character. These endings are hints that the process of selectivity involved in human mating and reproduction will, in the evolutionary course of life, be both physically and socially beneficial.

To Ellen Glasgow, the safest antidote for sentimental decay was a vantage point of skeptical detachment, and so it was to Stribling. His novels come to grips with the physical realities of life and present characters who are neither idealized nor abstracted. There are perhaps few of these characters that we can like or admire, probably because Stribling himself, in his creation of them, did not really like or admire them; but he did not dislike them. It was only by maintaining his position of the objective observer that he was able in his novels about the South, for example, to isolate those facets of southern society that have been basic in the development of that section since the Civil War. Like Dr. Fyke in *These Bars of Flesh,* Stribling was an experimenter — let the experiment come out as it will; for he himself was neutral. The result is literature that relies not on sentimentality, moral condemnation, nor technical innovation for its motive but on a detached point of view that is unyielding in its examination.

Combining keen insight and wide-open receptivity to the life around him with a penchant for intricately designed plots, Stribling produced a group of novels that are good reading and that record given social conditions at given times and places in history. Moreover, through those novels dealing with the South, he opened up a considerable amount of untouched material for southern writers who were to follow. Twenty years before Robert Penn Warren, he described southern politics and southern business life; before William Faulkner, he discovered the Negro as a victim, not a stage darkie; before Thomas Wolfe, he saw the southern town and its blighting effect on young men; and so on through many of the themes, motifs, and subjects of the southern renaissance.

As a pioneer in the southern renaissance, Stribling helped to force a new view of the South; and he helped to clear the way for those who would work in the area during the ensuing decades. In short, Thomas Sigismund Stribling helped to create modern southern literature; and in doing so, he earned for himself a place in the American literary chronicle.

# Notes and References

*Chapter One*

1. This quotation is from a series of taped conversations that I had with T. S. Stribling at his home in Clifton, Tennessee, on January 21 through 23, 1964. Hereafter referred to as Tape.

2. Tape.

3. Tape.

4. Tape.

5. The story goes that on one occasion, when Christopher Stribling was about to render a paddling to young Tom, the boy shouted that surely his father would not want to be known for spanking a son for wanting to learn to write. Christopher was so struck by this statement that he never again threatened Tom with a whipping for writing.

6. T. S. Stribling, quoted in Charles C. Baldwin, *The Men Who Make Our Novels* (New York, 1924), p. 465.

7. Tape.

8. Tape.

9. Tape.

10. Tape.

11. T. S. Stribling, quoted in Baldwin, p. 470.

12. *Ibid.*, p. 469.

13. *Ibid.*, p. 471.

14. T. S. Stribling in Ulysses Walsh, "Read and Write and Burn," *The Writer* XLV (May, 1932), 126.

15. Tape.

16. W. J. Cash, *The Mind of the South* (New York, 1941), p. 146.

17. Thomas Nelson Page, *Red Riders* (New York, 1924), p. 14.

18. Thomas Nelson Page, quoted in Robert Spiller, *et al.*, *Literary History of the United States* (New York, 1946), p. 849.

19. Francis Butler Simkins, "The South," in *Regionalism in America*, ed. Merrill Jensen (Madison, Wis., 1951), p. 148.

20. T. S. Stribling, "Southern Verse," *Poet Lore* XVII (Winter, 1906), 104 - 5.

21. Louis D. Rubin, "Notes on a Rear-Guard Action," in *The Idea of the South*, ed. Frank Vandiver (Houston, 1963), p. 30.

22. John Bradbury, *Renaissance in the South* (Chapel Hill, N. C., 1963), p. 3.

23. Tape.

## Chapter Two

1. Simkins in Jensen, p. 149.

2. Harlan Hatcher, *Creating the Modern American Novel* (New York, 1935), pp. 144 - 45.

3. T. S. Stribling to a Mr. Kane, quoted in Desda Garner, "An Intimate Study of the Life and Writings of T. S. Stribling" (M. A. thesis, Peabody College for Teachers, 1934), p. 14.

4. *Birthright* (New York, 1922), p. 82. Subsequent page references are noted in parentheses in the text.

5. "The Author of *Birthright* Replies," quoted in Garner, p. 24.

## Chapter Three

1. *Fombombo* (New York, 1923), p. 24. Subsequent page references are cited in parentheses in the text.

2. *Red Sand* (New York, 1924), p. 39. Subsequent page references are cited in parentheses in the text.

## Chapter Four

1. *Teeftallow* (New York, 1926), p. 1. Subsequent page references are cited in parentheses in the text.

2. Sinclair Lewis, *Babbitt* (New York, 1961), p. 5.

3. The Scopes trial was held in Dayton, Tennessee, the same year that Stribling was working on *Teeftallow*. He said in one of our conversations that he felt the inclusion of this passage and the one on pp. 25 and 26 dated the novel and that that was really a bad thing. He was well aware that he "pegged" his novels on specific social situations and that, as a result, they lacked universality.

## Chapter Five

1. *Bright Metal* (Garden City, 1928), p. 3. Subsequent page references are cited in parentheses in the text.

2. *Backwater* (Garden City, 1930), p. 253. Subsequent page references are cited in parentheses in the text.

## Chapter Six

1. T. S. Stribling, Interview in *Clarion Ledger* (Jackson, Miss.), November 1, 1931.

2. *The Forge* (Garden City, 1931), p. 1. Subsequent page references are cited in parentheses in the text.

3. T. S. Stribling, quoted by Garner, p. 107.

### Chapter Seven

1. *The Store* (New York, 1932), p. 65. Subsequent page references are cited in parentheses in the text.
2. Tape.

### Chapter Eight

1. Anonymous, *New York Times,* May 4, 1933, p. 30.
2. *The Unfinished Cathedral,* (New York, 1934), pp. 1 - 2. Subsequent page references are cited in parentheses in the text.
3. "The Author's Store," *Wings* VI (July, 1932), 17.
4. In a letter to me (April 29, 1964) in which she described the years she and Stribling spent in Florida, Lou Ella Stribling wrote: "There were a number of Koreshians in Fort Myers. They were all rather intellectual and cultivated in the arts and music. I guess I said 'and music' because I put it in a place of its own among the arts." There is evidence in the trilogy that Stribling identified himself with Jerry Catlin II. Jerry, for example, marries Aurelia at about the same age that Stribling married Lou Ella. Aurelia's love of music parallels that of Lou Ella, and the effect of Aurelia's playing on Catlin seems similar to that of Lou Ella's on Stribling.
5. In our conversations, Stribling made a passing comment that miscegenation was an attempt on the part of the human race to improve itself.
6. T. .S. Stribling, quoted in Halford Luccock, *American Mirror: Social, Ethical, and Religious Aspects of American Literature 1930 - 1940* (New York, 1940), p. 72.
7. T. S. Stribling, *Florence Herald,* May 25, 1934.

### Chapter Nine

1. *The Sound Wagon* (New York, 1936), p. 90. Subsequent page references are cited in parentheses in the text.
2. *These Bars of Flesh* (New York, 1938), p. 18. Subsequent page references are cited in parentheses in the text.

### Chapter Ten

1. T. S. Stribling's epitaph.
2. Anonymous, *Florence Times,* January 10, 1964.
3. T. S. Stribling, quoted in Ralph Morrissey, "You Can Go Home Again," *Nashville Tennessean,* December 28, 1952, p. 18.
4. Louis D. Rubin, *The Faraway Country* (Seattle, 1963), p. 14.
5. *Ibid,* p. 15.
6. Tape.
7. T. S. Stribling, quoted in "America's Town Meeting of the Air," December 26, 1935, p. 20.
8. *Ibid.,* p. 24.
9. *Teeftallow,* p. 110.

# Selected Bibliography

PRIMARY SOURCES

This checklist is as complete as I have been able to make it. T. S. Stribling did not have a record of his hundreds of Sunday-school stories, and I have made no attempt to list them.

1. Novels

*The Cruise of the Dry Dock*. Chicago: Reilly, Britton, 1917.
*Birthright*. New York: Century, 1922. First published serially in *Century Magazine* in 1921.
*East Is East*. New York: Frank A. Munsey Co., 1922.
*Fombombo*. New York: Century, 1923.
*Red Sand*. New York: Harcourt, Brace, 1924.
*Teeftallow*. Garden City, N.Y.: Doubleday, Page, 1926.
*Bright Metal*. Garden City, N.Y.: Doubleday, Doran, 1928.
*Strange Moon*. Garden City, N.Y.: Doubleday, Doran, 1929.
*Backwater*. Garden City, N.Y.: Doubleday, Doran, 1930.
*The Forge*. Garden City, N.Y.: Doubleday, Doran, 1931.
*The Store*. Garden City, N.Y.: Doubleday, Doran, 1932.
*The Unfinished Cathedral*. Garden City, N.Y.: Doubleday, Doran, 1934.
*The Sound Wagon*. Garden City, N.Y.: Doubleday, Doran, 1935.
*These Bars of Flesh*. Garden City, N.Y.: Doubleday, Doran, 1938.

2. Collection of Short Stories

*Clues of the Caribbees*. Garden City, N.Y.: Doubleday, Doran, 1929.

3. Short Stories

"House of the Haunted Shadows." Unknown grocery-store pamphlet, 1893.
"The Web of the Sun." *Adventure Magazine*, sometime before 1917.
"Passing of the St. Louis Bearcat." *Everybody's Magazine*, Dec., 1919.
"What a Young Man Should Know." *Everybody's Magazine*, Jan., 1921.
"Native Stock." *Pictorial Review*, July, 1925.
"A Passage to Benares." *Adventure Magazine*, Feb., 1926.

"It Don't Mean Nothin' to Men." *Pictorial Review*, Oct., 1926.
"Bride." *Women's Home Companion*, Dec., 1926.
"Mating of Pompalone." *Golden Book*, June, 1927.
"Nebo." *Adventure Magazine*, May, 1930.
"Nogglesby." *Adventure Magazine*, June, 1930.
"The Resurrection of Chin Lee." *Adventure Magazine*, April, 1932.
"Bullets." *Adventure Magazine*, May, 1932.
"There Are Men Like That." *Collier's*, Oct. 29, 1932.
"The Cablegram." *Adventure Magazine*, Nov., 1932.
"She Had Hair Like Her Sister's." *Delineator*, June, 1933.
"Guileford." *Pictorial Review*, Aug., 1933.
"Fan Mail." *Delineator*, Sept., 1934.
"H. Ah. A." *Saturday Evening Post*, Jan. 26, 1935.
"Next Year." *Saturday Evening Post*, March 2, 1935.
"Miss Jacksburg." *Saturday Evening Post*, May 18, 1935.
"Certificate." *Saturday Evening Post*, June 22, 1935.
"Afternoon Performance." *Saturday Evening Post*, Feb. 26, 1936.
"Fixers." *Saturday Evening Post*, April 25, 1936.
"Easement." *Saturday Evening Post*, June 6, 1936.
"Oil and the Building Fund." *Saturday Evening Post*, Feb. 27, 1937.
"Issaquena Goes Grateful." *Saturday Evening Post*, April 3, 1937.
"Chandler Chooses." *Saturday Evening Post*, May 8, 1937.
"More Looks than Brains." *McCall's*, Oct., 1937.
"Gone with the Rain." *Saturday Evening Post*, Feb. 12, 1938.
"Yankees Don't Know Nothin'." *Saturday Evening Post*, June 18, 1938.
"Quasibottomy." *Saturday Evening Post*, March 25, 1939.
"My Cousin Ji-um." *Saturday Evening Post*, Jan. 3, 1942.
"The Mystery of the Chief of Police." *Ellery Queen*, July, 1945.
"The Mystery of the Paper Wad." *Ellery Queen*, Jan., 1946
"The Mystery of the Sock and the Clock." *Ellery Queen*, Jan., 1946.
"Count Jalacki Goes Fishing." *Ellery Queen*, Sept., 1946.
"A Note to Count Jalacki." *Ellery Queen*, Oct., 1946.
"Mystery of the 81st Kilometer Stone." *Ellery Queen*, July, 1947.
"The Mystery of the Seven Suicides." *Ellery Queen*, April, 1948.
"A Daylight Adventure." *Ellery Queen*, March, 1950.
"The Mystery of the Personal Ad." *Ellery Queen*, May, 1950.
"The Mystery of the Choir Boy." *Ellery Queen*, Jan., 1951.
"The Mystery of Andorus Enterprises." *Ellery Queen*, Sept., 1951.
"The Mystery of the Half-Painted House." *Ellery Queen*, April, 1952.
"Death Deals Diamonds." *Famous Detective*, Nov., 1952.
"Figures Don't Die." *Famous Detective*, Feb., 1953.
"Dead Wrong." *Smashing Detective Stories*, March, 1953.
"The Warning on the Lawn." *Ellery Queen*, March, 1953.
"The Mystery of the Five Money Orders." *Ellery Queen*, March, 1954.
"The Telephone Fisherman." *Ellery Queen*, Jan., 1955.

"Murder at Flowtide." *Saint Detective,* March, 1955.
"The Case of the Button." *Saint Detective,* Sept., 1955.

SECONDARY SOURCES

1. Books

BALDWIN, CHARLES C. *The Men Who Make Our Novels.* New York: Dodd, Mead, 1924. A general look at how a number of novelists of the early 1920s view their craft, including Stribling.

BRADBURY, JOHN M. *Renaissance in the South.* Chapel Hill, N.C.: University of North Carolina Press, 1963. A comprehensive survey of the many writers who contributed to the southern literary renaissance, including brief references to Stribling.

DAVIDSON, DONALD. *The Spyglass.* Edited by John Tyree Fain. Nashville: Vanderbilt University Press, 1963. A collection of Davidson's book reviews, including one on *Teeftallow.*

HATCHER, HARLAN. *Creating the Modern American Novel.* New York: Farrar and Rinehart, 1935. A study of the American novel of the time, containing brief commentaries on Stribling's treatment of the Negro in *Birthright, The Forge, The Store,* and *The Unfinished Cathedral.*

HOFFMAN, ARTHUR SULLIVANT, ed. *Fiction Writers and Fiction Writing.* Indianapolis: Bobbs-Merrill, 1923. Interviews with selected novelists including Stribling, on their approaches to their art.

LUCCOCK, HALFORD. *American Mirror: Social, Ethical, and Religious Aspects of American Literature, 1930 - 1940.* New York: Macmillan, 1940. A broad approach to American literature of the 1930s, with minor references to Stribling.

MOSES, MONTROSE. *The Literature of the South.* New York: Crowell, 1910. A general survey of southern literature and its development.

RUBIN, LOUIS. D. *The Faraway Country.* Seattle: University of Washington Press, 1963. A series of essays on major modern southern writers and their contributions to the southern literary renaissance.


2. Articles and Reviews

BATES, ERNEST. "Thomas Sigismund Stribling." *English Journal* XXVI (Feb., 1935), 91 - 100. A general treatment of Stribling and his works to that time.

DICKENS, BYROM. "T. S. Stribling and the South." *Sewanee Review* XLII (July - Sept., 1934), 341 - 49. An overview of Stribling's work through *The Unfinished Cathedral,* pinpointing the themes of the various novels as they relate to the South.

ECKLEY, WILTON. "T. S. Stribling: Pioneer in the Southern Renaissance." *Iowa English Yearbook* (Fall, 1966), pp. 47 - 54. A general discussion of the themes of Stribling's novels as they contributed to the southern literary renaissance.

TATE, ALLEN. "T. S. Stribling." *Nation* CXXXVIII (June 20, 1934), 709. A
    negative and rather biased review of *The Unfinished Cathedral*.
WALSH, ULYSSES. "Read and Write and Burn." *Writer* XLV (May, 1932),
    127 - 29. An interview with Stribling discussing his methods of
    writing.
WARREN, ROBERT PENN. "T. S. Stribling: A Paragraph in the History of
    Realism." *American History* II (Feb., 1934), 463 - 86. A negative
    analysis of *Bright Metal, Teeftallow, The Forge, The Store,* and *The
    Unfinished Cathedral*.

3. Interview

ECKLEY, WILTON. Interview with T. S. Stribling, January 21 - 23, 1964, Clif-
    ton, Tennessee. A taped interview in which Stribling talked on various
    aspects of his writing and his views on life. In addition to the original,
    there is a copy of the tape among the Stribling papers in Clifton.

# Index

(The works of Stribling are listed under his name)

123

95484

**DATE DUE**

| | | | |
|---|---|---|---|
| | | | |
| | | | |
| | | | |
| | | | |
| | | | |
| | | | |
| | | | |
| | | | |
| | | | |
| | | | |
| | | | |
| | | | |